BLOGGING
through
THE OBAMA YEARS

Richard Miner

TABLE OF CONTENTS

Introduction vii

Chapter 1 Mythic America

Introduction 3

So What's With Barack Obama 4

Obama versus McCain 11

Is It Personalities, Myth, or Both? 17

Myth in America 23

Hard Right 31

Chapter 2 Democracy or Either/Or

Introduction 41

Liberal Conservative 43

The Chicken or the Egg? 49

Political Ads? Forget About It 57

Chapter 3 Larger Government—Get Used to It

Introduction 65

Energy Independence? Nonsense 67

Questions for Democratic Presidential Candidates 69

Milton Friedman 101 73

Friedman 102 78

Praise for a Real American Victory 83

President Obama's First Week 86

Our Congressional Representatives 90

Interview with Representative Leonard Lance 96

It's One Country 104

Chapter 4   Our Place in the New World Order

Introduction. 113

So What's a Democrat to Do? 115

Message to Barack Obama. 119

US Economy: Larger Picture 121

Arab Democracy?. 126

Chapter 5   Middle Class Revival

Introduction. 133

Inconceivable 135

Solidarity Forever. 147

Chapter 6   Healthcare

Introduction. 159

The Public Option and the Mandate 161

Healthcare Update 171

Responses to Healthcare Blog Entries 179

Angry Letter to my Representative,

After Healthcare Vote. 186

Republican Healthcare Plan. 188

Chapter 7   Education

Introduction. 197

Childhood Left Behind 198

Chapter 8   Bank Bailout and Stimulus

Introduction. 209

What Next Obama?. 211

Financial Bailout 217

Financial Regulation 221

Chapter 9 Guns

Introduction. 227

Back from Vacation 231

Representative Mike Ferguson Responds 237

The Second Amendment 239

Give Me Liberty, No Wait, Give Us an Army. 242

Chapter 10 Final Thoughts

Introduction. 245

Letter to the Editor 246

Response to Letter to the Editor 248

Healthcare Debate? 251

Postscript 255

INTRODUCTION

November, 2011

I began blogging in early 2007 with a quite simple objective in mind. I wanted to see how my congressman, Michael Ferguson, 7th district, central New Jersey, voted on issues I considered important. I'd describe my district as centrist Republican; wealthy but with some areas that used to support a middle class industrial job base, now in decline.

To provide a check on my congressman's voting record, I also followed the corresponding votes of Rush Holt, a Democrat and liberal, who represented a district just to the south that includes Princeton and Trenton. Trenton's motto 'Trenton makes the world takes' indicates something about its past; Princeton could stand as a poster child for eastern intellectuals.

Fairly soon in the evolution of the blog I began to comment on what I thought about the votes. At some point, probably about the same time I began commenting, I convinced myself that I had the further objective of becoming a more informed citizen. I don't know about others, but I find I am often tempted to enhance whatever I'm doing with some nobler motive. Perhaps I should confess that in retirement writing was a congenial way to keep my mind active, one I preferred, along with choral music, to other possibilities. Over time, commenting on issues became primary, recording votes secondary, until the recording ceased altogether. Fortunately, at about the same time, I noticed that the Newark Star Ledger, my Jersey paper, was publishing the votes on major legislation for all of New Jersey's representatives.

Though my motives may not have been as noble as I might have imagined, the writing effort has produced results; I am a better informed citizen than I used to be. Of course, retirement gives me the time to read much more, to indulge political junky habits that went into a state of relative hibernation as I helped my wife raise children and as we both worked to support our family and to provide for a future that could include retirement.

Becoming a better informed citizen does not mean, and does not require, becoming an expert. We have lots of experts out there on every subject imaginable. Obviously no one person could become expert on every subject imaginable that might influence politics; citizens need to listen to experts and evaluate sources, but there is no requirement that citizens be experts on anything.

So, whatever I said in these blogs and this book was written as a citizen, not an expert. If, because I am not an expert, inaccuracies crept into my thinking, I can only apologize and try to learn from whatever commentary I receive or from any contradictory information I might come across as I continue to reconsider issues.

Because the book is meant to represent a series of blogs, written over nearly five years, and then warped into book form over one month, I decided there was good reason to leave thoughts, which may have been modified later, as they were when the blogs were written. I did occasionally, while revising, update footnotes and wording in the text. I tried not to change anything I thought at the date of each entry without making the updating clear.

I've provided further updating as introductions to each chapter, all dated November 2011. Those chapter introductions represent my most recent thoughts. These updates turned out to be one of the advantages of transforming a blog into a book with chapters. I got to rethink and summarize. I got to take into account more recent events.

Among the disadvantages of the transformation, I need to mention one; blogs are freer form thoughts that aren't meant to fit neatly into chapters. You'll find that sections of one blog could easily end up in any number of chapters. I got frustrated enough with this problem to mention my difficulties in one of the chapter introductions; apologies to the reader for any chapter placements that seem arbitrary.

One recent event that has set off some fundamental rethinking deserves mention. I stated often in my blog entries a belief in the power of effective government to balance the influences of other major power centers, like corporations, whatever those influences might be. I looked at two major power centers, government and corporate America, as metaphorically occupying much of the political power space; increase one and, as if the space can't stand a vacuum of power, the other devours the void. The Occupy Wall Street movement argues that any balance I may have imagined actually existing has been systemically eliminated.

Citizens should be the overwhelming shakers and movers behind government. Whatever they think about issues, they can act in many ways to direct government action; they can vote, for example, they can organize, they can protest, and they can write. Their influence over corporations is hardly equivalent. They can't vote for the board of directors; protests can have only limited effect. What the Occupy movements argue is that citizens now have little if any more influence over government than they do over corporations, in great part because corporation money has taken the citizens' representatives in government away from them.

Taking government back is behind both the Occupy movements and the Tea Party. As Lawrence Lessig[1], Harvard University professor, recently argued during a Charlie Rose interview, one solution is to take the corrupting source of money out of the electoral process. We need a level of commitment to democracy that would allow us to absorb the cost of campaigning rather than leaving that cost to those who funnel money from corporations or any other source of power in various legal, surreptitious, and

---

[1] See Lawrence Lessig, Republic Lost: How Money Corrupts Congress—and a Plan to Stop It

outright illegal ways through K-Street to our, that's our, representatives.

Unfortunately, as Lawrence Lessig points out, our representatives aren't about to change standard operating procedures any time soon, and it will take time to mount sufficient pressure, even if the Occupy movement and the Tea Party unite on this one objective. In the meantime I'll stick with my instant solution described in 'Political Ads—Forget About It'. That's 'forget about it' with a Bronx accent and a Bronx cheer thrown in. Just shut those ads off and find other ways to become an informed citizen. Think of all that corporate money K-Street would waste if no one listened to the babble their money buys.

CHAPTER 1
Mythic America

Introduction

November, 2011

I've come to think that the way we make political decisions involves a complex interaction of logic, myth, emotion, personal preference, and any number of cues[2] that attach a candidate to us or to what we believe for whatever reason. In this chapter I've collected entries that express my frustrations as I tried to develop my ideas about why people vote as they do. David Brooks, regular New York Times op-ed, conservative contributor, has developed similar ideas over the years, and his input to my thoughts will be obvious to his readers.

The troubling part derives from what most of us believe about our own political thought processes. We believe (and especially I believe) that we approach politics by examining the facts and acting logically. Of course that's exactly what I do, but what could so many of you out there be doing that leads you to such illogical conclusions? What could such a careful intellect as David Brooks be thinking to come up with such contrary views? Needless (I hope) to say, I needed to reconsider my own political decision making processes, too.

---

[2] See the entry 'Inconceivable' Chapter 5.

So What's With Barack Obama

July 16, 2008

Over the last month or so, as Barack Obama has begun to craft the broader appeal necessary to win a general election as opposed to the Democratic primary, progressives have become increasingly nervous over what appear to be a number of modifications to positions they may have assumed (rightly or wrongly) that he held. The shifts, modifications, refinements, (or whatever term you like) have given me pause too.

Popular explanations fall into several categories. He's a consummate politician, with skills honed in Chicago no less; he knows the game. Or, unlike our current president, he looks at problems without ideological blinders so as events change, modifications are inevitable. He thinks with a relatively open mind. There's not much point in thinking if thinking doesn't occasionally lead to a new position. Or, he's a flip-flopper without sound principles, willing to shift positions merely to gain tactical advantage by appealing to issue groups he needs to win.

As a Barack supporter, now (after first Edwards and then Hillary were defeated), I'm in the 'he thinks' camp. Just the way he speaks, the syntax he is capable of handling, indicates to me the ability to look at events and consider options intelligently and logically. I think he won't start with the answers and fit the facts to them, as Bush and company so often have. I think he won't need to surround himself with ideologues, unanimously supporting the same ideology. He's not so insecure in his ability to think that having people around who may bring with them different perspectives would seem like a threat; he won't need to emphasize loyalty above honesty, as the current administration has. For me there is nothing more important than a president who can consider differing views while forming his own. Our problems are complex; single-minded answers won't do.

That said, I still find myself sifting through his positions and modifications, looking for his core direction. I'm evaluating him in part by trying to figure where I would compromise and where I wouldn't. I am trying to isolate those areas where I feel strongly enough not to compromise before I get too upset about what may appear to be his compromises. As I think about this, I've found lots of areas where I surprise myself by just how far I am willing to reconsider positions I thought I had settled, for myself at least.

Environmental issues seem to be one area where my settled opinions are less secure than I would have believed possible as little as a couple of months ago. I find myself listening to the possibility that off shore drilling may be necessary, putting me to the right of Arnold and the New York Times. Who'd have thunk?

I've arrived at this disturbing position by two routes. First, I've been upset for a long time with 'NIMBY' progressives who won't even support off shore windmills, let alone oil wells, if they appear as thumbnail size impediments to their view from Nantucket. I love the Cape and the islands too, but for windmills, I'd bear with a slight change in perspective. In fact I like the sight of windmills. So, if for good reasons I came to think we need more oil, I'd be hard put to make the argument that they should be in someone else's back yard rather than my own. I couldn't say no to oil rigs 100 miles off the Jersey shore just because they might not look nice.

But, unlike windmills, appearance is not the chief argument against oil rigs. Oil slicks on the Jersey shore would upset me. I'd need much more proof of the need for more oil to allow me to consider the need to take pollution risks, despite attempts of advocates to minimize those risks. So, do we need more oil or don't we? I just heard an interesting factoid from Fareed Zakaria on NPR. American SUVs use about 10 million barrels of oil a day, 3 to 4 times the total use for India. We may be able to blame others for oil shortages to some degree now and the degree may increase, but for immediate benefits I'm convinced that a Hummer scrap heap would serve us better than any emphasis either on increased supply or on trying to influence the usage patterns of up and coming economies like India and China. Fortunately American citizens aren't waiting for government action; they're sending those awful monsters off to scrap pronto.

That said, I do think that, if we established a long term energy plan that seriously emphasized conservation, provided for a Manhattan Project sized sustainable energy program, and initiated an intelligent mass transit system, I'd think about off shore oil drilling as a stopgap measure to get us through the next 20 to 50 years or so with less trauma than we may otherwise experience. I'd be against leaving the decision to the states (sorry Arnold, but that Bush decision needs congressional revision); this is a national issue, and where we drill should be a national decision based on environmental evaluations. On an environmental basis, Anwar (Alaska) is clearly the worst place to drill (and the first place we would drill if the decision were left to states); NJ and California are probably worse than the Gulf. Letting the states decide means we don't consider the environment as the primary factor; we leave it to the greed of regional politics or to a local concentration of NIMBYs (understandable as NIMBY concerns may be in this case).

Obama seems to have maintained his opposition to off shore drilling. Unless I missed something, his opposition remains unnuanced. His web site does outline the long-term plans for a sensible energy policy that would make a change in this position a reasonable refinement, as long as he indicated that off shore oil would serve only as a temporary cushion. A change of that sort would not necessarily be a flip-flop or a politically expedient tactic; it could be based on an honest re-evaluation. It would be just the sort of change I'd be willing to see him make. I don't see any danger of Obama slipping any further by suggesting that more oil is a real, long term answer.

What troubles me a bit about his environmental stance is what seems to be an emphasis on ethanol. Obama's web site clearly shows that he understands the limitations of corn ethanol, which returns two gallons while using one to produce. Sugar cane returns an eight to one advantage, better; but unfortunately both options consume land that might either produce food or serve us better as reserved forest land. At best, as the web site makes quite clear, we should look at something like cellulosic ethanol from sources like sorghum, wheat or rice straw, Bush's switch grass, paper pulp, etc. where the material used for fuel production is a throw-away and the crop or main product remains usable.

Even so the whole idea of using renewable fuels to replace fossil fuels seems like yet another temporary solution. Even cellulosic crops require land to grow, and as the demand grows they too might well lead to encroachments upon land the world will need just to feed people or of the remaining forests needed to preserve biodiversity or of buffer lands needed to contain farm pollutants and control floods. The Europeans are in the process of changing their minds on ethanol in general, and we will have to change too.

Again, I'd give Obama a pass on ethanol if he'd place it down on the list of solutions a bit and describe it as the stopgap measure it is. The web site does warn that even cellulosic ethanol can't do much more than replace a small percentage of expected usage and the site does mention the downsides.

What gets me more upset are the constitutional issues he's muffed recently. Anyone who reads my blog knows how I feel about the 2nd amendment. How someone as informed in constitutional law as Obama could support the NRA myth that an amendment about militias confers individual rather than collective rights is a mystery to me. I'd expect such distortions of the founders' intent from the likes of Thomas, Scalia, Souter, or Roberts, but from Obama, what got into him? I simply can't believe that he really supports that decision.

The only explanation that makes sense to me is that he needs the votes of the gun folks and that he thinks they are unable to understand that individual gun possession does not require a constitutional level protection. Still, though I feel strongly on this one and I feel strongly that NJ's tough gun laws ought to be nationalized; I'm willing to let the overall issue play itself out in congress and the courts. I'm sure enough that despite his constitutional glibness on this issue, he'll appoint judges more likely to get it right than McCain will. Just read McCain on gun rights. Every police officer in the country ought to. AK47's are ok with him. So Obama gets a qualified pass on this one.

The recent FISA (Foreign Intelligence Surveillance Act) revision vote troubles me even more. All I can say is that the choices presented in the vote were tough, so tough that I'm not sure how I would have voted. Of course I'd like to see a clear stand against wiretaps without warrants, but that wasn't one of the choices. Somehow we've panicked ourselves so severely over the nut in the cave that the courageous option isn't even on the table anymore.

What Obama needed to decide was whether the Bush administration's illegal interpretation of the original FISA bill was preferable to a slightly more controlled version of the wiretap procedure. Given that slim and ugly choice, I'd probably vote for it. But, where's the protest against such a choice? I'll have to check the Obama website to see if he protests. I'm with the Libertarians on this one, but I wonder where Obama really is. A single sentence on the web site promising to allow better access to congressional committees about FISA decisions doesn't reassure me anymore than the current bill.

Really addressing the FISA issue requires us to look at how we are dealing with terrorism. Central to that discussion is the sloppy term our president used to describe our response. Calling it a war is almost as inaccurate as calling our problems with drugs a war on drugs. Wars are fought against countries with governments that can fall. Terrorists and drug dealers are not official state entities that can sign peace agreements ending hostilities. Wars lead to victories or defeats; let's just face it, terrorism and drug dealing will be with us probably forever.

We need to think of these problems long term, and we need to set up strategies that can hold up over the long term. Gutting constitutional rights to privacy is an ugly long-term policy. It's like restrictions on Habeas Corpus; we simply can't let these extreme 'war time' measures become permanent. Obama does 'strongly support' restoration of Habeas Corpus. McCain's web site reassurances that he will protect basic rights are so general that neither FISA nor Habeas Corpus is mentioned[3].

So, on the invasion of privacy issue I'd like to see something from Obama to assure me that he understands more fully. I suppose it's too much to ask that he drop war from his description of our reaction to terror, but at least I'd like to see a lot more emphasis on non-military reactions. Yes, I know he talks about negotiation with allies and those we have come to see as non-allies. That's fine. But, I'd like a direct acknowledgement in a major speech that we need to face the long-term nature of the problem. The issue is not whether we get troops out of Iraq in 16 months; the issue is what we do over the 8 years of his presidency to prepare ourselves to deal with a long lasting, perhaps endless, problem.

My own belief is that we need to start by preparing ourselves for a much different relationship with the rest of the world. We need to drop the superpower designation before we go broke paying for a superpower military. We are one strong nation among many strong nations (and far too many weak ones). Our

---

[3] He (McCain) will ensure that the war against terrorists is fought intelligently, with patience and resolve, using all instruments of national power. Moreover, he will lead this fight with the understanding that to impinge on the rights of our own citizens or restrict the freedoms for which our nation stands would be to give terrorists the victory they seek.

big problems—the environment, terror, resources, survival—are global, and we will need whatever any country can contribute to craft solutions. We can contribute substantially, but we need to recognize that there will be times when others lead. If we lead we need to lead while keeping our values and our freedoms intact.

Obama could say all this better than I can, and I'm waiting before I give him a pass on FISA. Here, he holds onto my support only because McCain shows no signs of having any more of a clue than President Bush. Talk about folks left behind in cold war thinking, that's McCain; Reagan could have written his web site section on security. I'll not allow my vote to send us backwards for another 4 to 8 years, after suffering the bankrupt thinking of the neo-conservatives over the last 8 years.

Obama versus McCain

September 8, 2008

Despite the post convention excitement about Sarah Palin, the newcomer on the vice presidential scene, this race should be about Obama and McCain. Of course if we were to continue talking about Palin, I'd prefer to hear more about her stand on the issues and a bit less about her glasses and about whatever resemblance she has to a pit bull. (One of the sweetest dogs I know is our daughter's pit bull, but that really is beside the point).

I'm hoping that citizens are talking more about the issues than the personalities, but if they are following the media lead, it's hard to imagine that they would be. The drone about personalities (from Obama's elitism or messianic qualities to McCain's temper or maverick instincts) has just about convinced me that maybe I need to reevaluate my own preference for issue discussions. Maybe the media knows its public, and maybe issues don't matter as much as I think they should. Maybe it is more important to know that Palin can handle an AK47 with aplomb than whether she has any idea what such a weapon on 42nd Street might mean to the NYC police force.

If we must spend most of our time on personalities, let's at least do it with some sense of why we are concentrating on these particular personalities. Obama and McCain are running for a really difficult executive office, and despite the media's love of sensational story telling for its own sake, if we are going to discuss their personalities, we ought to relate that discussion, as often as possible, to what we are electing them to do.

Whenever I think about an ideal presidential personality, I steal a book title[4] and think about FDR as the fox and the lion. Then, as I did in a previous blog entry, I add the prophet—the prophet, the fox, and the lion. Not many presidents have combined all three, Washington, Lincoln, Roosevelt, Kennedy, and (though it hurts me to say it) maybe even Reagan. Of course Reagan's prophesy gave us George Bush, so it pays to think about what's being prophesized, but then that's issue related, and we are not talking about issues.

Hillary Clinton stumbled into the prophetic quality when she praised Lyndon Johnson for the civil rights bills, but forgot to mention Martin Luther King, Jr.'s prophetic role in creating a public drive for that radical change, a long overdue change that altered our collective psyche. The prophet comes first; he or she has 'the vision thing' that both Bush presidents so obviously lacked.

Prophets not only have the vision, they have the ability to excite the citizenry about that vision. Democracy requires that any fundamental change begin with a sea change in the outlook of its citizenry before any decisive legislative action can take place. Democracy is a slow and frustrating system as seen from the viewpoint of those who share the vision; a sensible and cautious system to those who either don't share it or are slow to respond for whatever reason. But, if you are seeking real change, democracy has it right. Real change comes from the people changing and flows upward to a government that must finally respond or lose office.

Hands down Obama has the prophetic quality over McCain. All McCain offers are visions of the cowboy coming to town and blazing away at corruption. Certainly the citizenry is ready for that task after Tom Delay, Ralph Reed, Jack Abramoff, Ted Stevens, along with a host of less obvious scoundrels have dominated the news for the last 5 or 6 years. Citizens would need to be ready and fully behind any message McCain offered because he is far from

---

[4] Roosevelt: The Lion and the Fox, James MacGregor Burns. (It's a good read.)

an inspirational messenger. The convention message I heard from him, John the Lone Ranger (with Sarah as Tonto?) bravely doing battle against such an obvious and perennial target as corruption is not a prophetic message. And, if it were, McCain's limited ability to inspire wouldn't sell it.

Obama is all about mobilization against the odds, in part because his message strikes much of the public as impossibly ideal, just as real rights for blacks in the fifties and sixties did. I'm old enough to remember the political climate Martin Luther King, Jr. faced. Obama's message may not be as audacious as King's but it is audacious enough; he's telling us that we can drive our government toward better decisions and that government can actually make our lives better. A good portion of the US public believes that driving a stake into the heart of the government beast is the best solution; Bush and McCain both feed off that anger. Prophets don't feed off existing anger; they defy conventional opinion and then fight uphill battles against the people they anger by doing so.

Convincing Americans that they can believe again in their government, see it as on their side, that's a challenge in need of a prophet. Obama does not present himself as a lone crusader who can change our attitude toward government all by himself; he emphasizes our part in the movement. He will either convince us that we can face real problems and demand real solutions from Washington and get those solutions implemented, or he fails. If we do believe and if we do insist on real solutions, Washington will follow us, he says; if we don't, he loses and we all lose.

Talk about gambles, McCain's gamble, selecting an unknown Sarah Palin, is small potatoes compared to the chances Obama is taking. Obama's gamble is that he can convince enough of his fellow citizens that government can work when purveyors of conventional wisdom, all too firmly, say it can't. The task Obama has set for himself will take all his considerable speaking talent and, yes, all his star status. McCain belittles that star status because like the Bushes he does not understand its importance in inspiring people to believe in themselves and their country.

The prophet inspires; the fox implements. President Johnson was the ultimate fox. He knew how to work within the political system to get things done. A fox doesn't over-power the opposition. He listens, he understands, he cajoles, he drops hints, he backs off or back tracks, then moves forward (cautiously or sometimes not so cautiously), feints one way then another. We may not all care to remember, but Roosevelt got us to accept our role in WWII in part by making a number of foxy, tactical moves. Many Americans were hearty isolationists, against foreign entanglements. Cleverness, foxiness is an underrated quality but as necessary today as it was before WWII, once inspiration has readied the public for action. Of course you have to watch foxes carefully, or they pull off a skunky move like the Tonkin Gulf escapade.

The president needs to inspire and maneuver the public, but he needs to manage too. Working in the software industry, where people change from one company to another a lot, I've experienced my share of management styles. Just to mention the extremes, there's management by coercion and fear, and there is management by consensus. I've experienced both styles and several in between. Management by fear produces decisions that are foreordained by those with the power. People are afraid to speak out, afraid even to speak on the phone, they fear bugs, they fear for their jobs. They are belittled or dismissed when they disagree. Think Rumsfeld and Cheney. We've had enough of that style over the last 8 years, and it has cost us dearly.

Management by consensus is a bit of a misnomer because the manager ought to have a general idea of where he's headed, but he encourages others to speak openly, add ideas, oppose without serious consequences, and eventually consensus develops around general principles but with lots of information and input to modify and even correct the outcome. Management by consensus is foxy. The manager needs to hold back a bit and give others room. He or she needs to let others come up with ideas and then give them the sense that they came up with ideas you, as manager, will honestly consider. You don't make final decisions before you have in front of you honestly given information from as many involved persons as possible.

So far, I believe that Barack is more likely to tend toward consensus management than McCain. McCain's legendary temper doesn't bode well for those under him who might insist on a different view. He does seem to work fairly well with Democratic opponents in the senate when views are to a great extent shared. That makes him a party maverick and an independent thinker from the perspective of die-hard conservatives. He's foxy enough to reach consensus with equals, but I'm not sure I'd want to work for him. The advertised McCain is the one who sticks to his principles no matter what. We hear little about nuanced changes in those opinions as conditions change. I've always thought that changed opinions are the mark of any thinking person, else why think. Obama does change opinions, and you can question his motives for doing so, as I have, but for the most part his changes are well reasoned and nuanced. They show all the signs of the kind of careful consideration so woefully lacking over the last eight years.

If McCain has an obvious strength over Obama, one is apt to see it in the lion phase. Once he has made a decision, especially if he sees it as a moral decision, as he often does, you need to keep out of the way of the teeth and claws. He's known as someone who will stand his ground. Of course it's not too hard to site instances where he hasn't, but 'giving in' runs counter to his whole life story. The story on Obama, on the other hand, is that he gives in too easily. Both stories are far too stark to be true. Barack cut his teeth on Chicago politicians, not a forgiving crowd. He wouldn't have survived without considerable grit. And McCain backed down on tax breaks for the wealthy and perhaps on Lieberman as VP. Lieberman would have been a lion's choice. Palin smells like a bad compromise to secure the right wing of his base.

I can't think of better shorthand for expressing the differences between the McCain and Obama styles of leadership than the refrains that dominated the audience reaction at the conventions. From McCain supporters we heard, either 'USA', 'USA', 'USA' or 'Drill here, drill now'. 'USA' strikes me as equivalent to chanting 'Mother' or 'Apple Pie', hard to argue with it, hard to figure out just where it leads. At least we know where 'drill here, drill now' leads, but it's such a narrow and minimal solution to a real problem, you have to wonder why they didn't shout 'natural gas from the USA' or 'sustainable energy now', both real solutions with a much better future.

The Obama refrain is strikingly different. 'Yes we can'. It's tied to the central theme of his campaign. 'Yes', emphasize the positive, not the negative, not fear. 'We', that's all of us coming together through the democratic process at its best, messy as it often is. 'Can', we can believe in solutions and accomplish what needs to be accomplished.

Is It Personalities, Myth, or Both?

September 11, 2008

Ok, I'm almost ready to capitulate entirely and jettison the notion that issues and ideas matter at all in elections. If Thomas Friedman can give up, as he did in his Times op-ed yesterday (Sept.10), then who am I to cling to such a notion. In fact, as someone who spent a good portion of his early life studying literature, I should know about the overwhelming power of stories to move us better than most.

I even have personal stories of my early, married life that move me to this day, have me melting in nostalgic reveries right now. There's the memories of my wife and myself both working low paying jobs with lots of overtime while raising our children, the unpaid property taxes, the day we disconnected the oil heat and attached the flue to a wood burning cook stove because we had no money for oil. We had no money to buy a power saw, so I gathered wood using a handsaw. We cooked on that stove, lighted it in the morning with coals from the highly efficient wood stove in the living room; mulligan stew sat for days on the back burner gathering this and that in the way of leftovers as it slowly simmered away. There were the vegetable gardens, the goats for milk, cheese, and whey lemonade, the Indian Runner ducks for eggs that made baking a joy, the chickens. We lived this life for years.

Well, as you can see, I could go on and on, and, in fact, would love to. By the time I'd really finished reminiscing, you'd have a story of Appalachian hill country poverty that would do for several episodes of 'Little House in the Hills'. Everything I've mentioned so far did happen, but that's not the point. To get at the point I need to isolate one picture in my mind, then go up and retrieve the actual photo.

I looked at the photo and found the exercise amusing. The mental picture has my wife and her good friend at the time standing in the back yard next to that wood cook stove, both pregnant, with stacks of home-canned goods all around. They both have long folksy dresses, and this is one fine mental construct of fertility. Well, the actual photo check has my wife and the friend along with the canned goods in the back yard; neither wife nor friend is pregnant. We did haul the stove out into the backyard (often too hot in the fall to can inside), but not that year. There is another picture that looks like an emblem of fertility—two women, one pregnant, one not, with one holding a melon; but it's my wife and my sister-in-law in Vermont, not the friend and not in our backyard. It's a melon, not home-canned goods.

So why did I merge all this together into one memory? I did that, I believe, because, like most people, I build my own stories based on patterns that are much larger than the individual stories themselves. Sometimes these patterns become so widespread that we call them myths. They are partly true, partly constructed, and, yes, partly false.

'Wait a minute', you might say, 'didn't you just tell us that everything really happened and you just reconstructed some of it?' Yes, but I haven't yet told you the whole story, I included only the details that fit the myth. Here's some that don't. Our parents were well off and willing to help with cars and little details like that, we didn't come from poverty. We were both college educated, and I'd already dropped out of a medical career I could have pursued, and I'd refused an unsolicited job offer working for an NYC ad agency. I'd decided not to continue a college teaching career. I wanted to finish my PhD thesis, now gathering dust in the attic; I didn't need the distraction of a real job.

In the late sixties and early seventies this sort of behavior made sense, believe it or not. It was part of two other functioning myths of the time, back to the earth and follow your soul. Could I help it that I was pouring my soul into the earth myth and into the influence of medieval visual constructs on Elizabethan drama, the subject of my dissertation? I'll have to dig that thing out and see if it is as good as I thought it was. I hear Carol saying, oh please, not that again.

Myths are tricky little devils, and sometimes it helps to clarify things—to check the photo or remember some inconvenient, less romantic truths. We could just leave them alone to percolate and to amuse old folks; if they're just personal myths, no harm done. But, when they are classic American myths that we all are tempted to use to help us navigate the present, letting them take on too much romantic unreality has serious consequences.

Over the last couple of months I've been studying America's war of 1812. At that time, the pesky little myth our leaders needed to deal with in order to put up a credible fight was the myth that the militia had banded together during the revolution as a group of honorable men inspired by shouts of "give me liberty or give me death". Washington quickly learned during the Revolution that such inspired patriots were ok for skirmishes but that high-minded folk tended to go home after a battle or two.[5] What he found he needed were men with skin in the game, so he cajoled congress into paying an army and promising land grants at the end of the war. Then he got soldiers who stuck it out long enough for the payoff, and even men who had shared enough tough times to became fiercely loyal to each other and their leader. But as the War of 1812 developed, that reality had little power over the militia myth. Most people who hadn't served over the long haul still believed in the militia's ability to stop the British once again, and the lesson needed to be learned all over.

---

[5] See—William F. Marina, "Militia, Standing Armies, and the Second Amendment" for a more sympathetic view of the militia during the revolution. He notes Washington's negative views but argues that the militia set up the final victory by waging successful guerilla warfare over the extent of the war.

I think the pesky little myth that still manages to hang over our own time is that central credo of rugged individualism. We never tire (and in fact shouldn't tire) of hearing about the pioneers who headed west—a wagon, a family, and an odd collection of possessions—in order to make their own way in the new land, without laws and without regulations. They kept going and going until they hit the Pacific Ocean, and then waves more came in search of golden dreams, and then not able to go any further west, they went North to Alaska, where the rugged individual myth retains a smidgeon of realty to this day. There are probably still mountain men in Alaska, bless their souls. And, you can still experience a travel adventure or two if you try driving to Alaska rather than flying or taking a cruise ship.

But let's face just a few little truths about this myth. Most of us travel long distances on highways built by our government, inspired by Eisenhower's vision of a national highway system. We stop at restaurants along the way, and only the more romantic amongst us get off and try to see what's left of old route 66 or the Natchez Trace. And, Alaska, full of rugged individualists; give me a break. 1/3 of Alaska's budget comes from the federal government, 1/3 from oil companies, and I would guess that a good portion of the other 1/3 comes from tourists seeking rugged individualists or at best the sports that make people feel that way for a couple of days.

Despite its place at the heart of our national myth, Alaska ain't the heartland. There is not a less American state in the union than Alaska. Does it have any inner-city that any other American state would recognize? No. Is it anything like mid western farm states? Why you would have to drill in Alaska just to plant a seed.[6] Is it like a mid-west industrial state, struggling with lost jobs? No way, it

---

[6] Actually Alaska does grow things. Took a look at the state agriculture site and noted in particular when fresh veggies are available. Their list is dominated by crops that I might plant in August or September in hopes of getting a second, fall harvest. These quick growers are locally available fresh in Alaska mostly in August and September, as a first crop, I assume. The exception is tomatoes, available June-August. I suspect

has no rust belt industry. It's a petro-state, awash in petro-dollars, free to give its citizens cash back just for being alive. Economically, it's more like Saudi Arabia or Russia than Kansas.

The governor of Alaska does not need to make the kind of hard decisions our governor here in New Jersey and in other states throughout the union need to make. No cutback in services, no selling state owned assets like turnpikes, no hard decisions, no new taxes needed. I think people who say Sarah Palin is 'just like me' actually might be able to run Alaska for a few months. I don't think they could run any other state. That we are thinking that a governor of Alaska could serve as Vice President for the other 49 states seems off the charts absurd to me.

Why, then, do so many Americans seem to think that this McCain choice is so hunky-dory? Well, she carries a gun, she kills and skins moose, she fights the good fight against homo-sexual books, disses the notion that global warming might be related to human activity like burning fossil fuels, she believes the religious doctrine of creationism ought to be taught in schools. (Does she think it ought to be taught in a science class?) She believes rape and incest victims should have no choice. Or, as I prefer to put it, she's pro back alley abortion for the poor, European abortions for the rich, not free choice for all. Just on these issues alone, I cannot imagine that one person who backed Hillary (as I did) could for one moment think of letting this woman anywhere near the presidency.

But then I seem to have forgotten again, the election has nothing to do with issues. That's where I started this entry. She appeals in large part because she comes from the state of Alaska, the last state in the union with a shred of a claim left to the myth of rugged individualism. And she really acts the rugged individual part well. She can say, with what her supporters see as utterly charming conviction, "I stood up alone against the boys' club." Or, "I stood

---

these are hot-house grown. The warmest month in Wasilla is July—average maximum temp. 69, average minimum temp. 48.

alone against my party." Or, "I rejected the bridge to nowhere."[7] Or, "when I get to Washington, I'll ride shotgun for McCain as we blow away all those corrupt earmark spenders, like the ones I encouraged to support my hometown of Wasilla." And, "when I'm done cleaning up, I'll help my side-kick McCain, ah, ah, ah"[8]; well what do you expect, real plans for the future from a myth?

---

[7] Well at least she did after the nasty media pointed out what a boondoggle it was.
[8] Obviously I'm putting words in her mouth here and in the next phrase . But I think I've captured the flavor.

Myth in America

November 8, 2010

As someone who prefers to think of himself as guided by reason, at least when making political or financial decisions, I'm not exactly sympathetic to those who seem to base such decisions too trustingly on popular myths or on what they would like to believe. On the other hand, I spent years studying literature, or, at least in part, studying the construction or manipulation of myths. In some portion of my world heroes inspire, trees talk to each other, weeds express eons of experience, and ravens are wise beyond my understanding.

If I can believe in trees, weeds, and ravens, then certainly there is room in my world view for even the most popular myths. In fact I believe we cannot exist as a coherent society without the myths we share; but, also, I think that those myths that remain stuck in a past that never existed are causing serious harm to our collective well-being.

Imagine if, as Americans, we didn't believe, to a healthy degree, that "(1) each of us is judged solely on her or his own merits; (2) we each have a fair opportunity to develop those merits". The quotation is Harlan Dalton's[9] description of the Horatio Alger myth so central to our sense of our best selves. Unfortunately, I think few would argue with Dalton's next point, that each of these statements is "to be charitable, problematic." We'd be hard put not to admit that in the real world, paraphrasing Dalton, this "variant on the rugged individualist ethos" ignores a host of other factors— "pedigree, race, class, background, gender, national origin, sexual orientation" that help determine individual success for most of us. Let's see, is the life of Frederick Douglass the only real world encapsulation of the myth? Maybe Barack Obama?

---

[9] Harlan Dalton, Professor of Law, Yale.

Most of us were brought up on the rugged individualist myth played out over and over on the screen in what we will all recognize as a classic western scene, the lone hero who arrives just in time to save the wagon train. The wagon train serves as the perfect foil to the lone hero; it's a group of people bonded together to accomplish a difficult trip. The wagon train, an ideal expression of collective action, is almost always attacked or in imminent danger of some form of destruction, when the rugged outcast or loner (John Wayne) comes riding to the rescue.

Somehow, those in the wagon train, folks who put together a social life and braved difficult if not quite impossible odds together, aren't up to whatever emergency is about to descend. They are often depicted as downright helpless, if not quite wimpy. Mountain men hold wagon trains and social life, for that matter, in disdain. Somehow the undercurrent of the myth often gets lost; after all, those in the wagon trains and the social instincts that they practiced won the west, while the mountain men ended up in Alaska suckling off the federal government and oil companies, shooting wolves from the safety of piper cubs while throwing punches at their benefactors in Washington. Man up, Sarah Palin.

We shouldn't be too surprised that such myths, as the oh-so digestible, rugged individualist myth, drive our politics these days. Such wondrously, delectable fantasies have driven our politics ever since we had politics. One of my favorites is the myth that drove Andrew Jackson's campaign of 1824, when somewhat miraculously, Jackson, the outsider, almost won the election against four other eminently qualified insiders. He won the popular vote. Of course the first US depression (1819), western anger toward the second US Bank (blood sucking easterners), and detestation of Washington insiders helped fire up his campaign. But, Jackson's popularity rested almost entirely on the famous Battle of New Orleans, where he and his brave Kentucky sharp shooters (think Daniel Boone types) beat an overwhelming, well trained force of redcoats. Ah, what a wonderful political poster it would have made. I can almost see it—square jawed, white haired Jackson, front and center, long rifled Kentucks, "half horse, half alligator"[10], filling the background.

Great political poster, completely inaccurate story. Here's what happened as I remember it from my historical readings (no, my grand-children, I wasn't there, personally). Jackson's main force bravely held the center, decimating the attacking redcoats with artillery, mostly, long rifles were secondary. The Kentucks were assigned to hold the right (or was it the left) flank. Unfortunately they arrived late and exhausted with inadequate supplies. The redcoats' attack against the Kentucks succeeded in routing them rather easily. I suspect most of us would have run if we faced the attack they did, with inadequate artillery and without sufficient

---

[10] But Jackson, he was wide awake,
And was not scared of trifles;
For well he knew what aim we take
With our Kentucky rifles;
He led us down to Cypress Swamp,
The ground was low and mucky;
There stood John Bull in pomp,
And here was old Kentucky.

A bank was rais'd to hide our breast,
Not that we thought of dying,
But then we always like to rest,
Unless the game is flying;
Behind it stood our little force
None wished it to be greater,
For ev'ry man was half a horse,
And half an alligator.

They found, at last, 'twas vain to fight,
Where lead was all the booty,
And so they wisely took to flight,
And left us all our beauty.
And now, if danger e'er annoys,
Remember what our trade is,
Just send for us Kentucky boys,
And we'll protect ye, ladies.

ammunition for those rifles. Jackson had no sympathy for them, however; he was outraged at their 'cowardice'.

It gets better, though; the force that did hold back the British in the center was made up of New Orleans residents—creoles, blacks, others, and get this, Lafitte's pirates, plus some of Jackson's Indian allies. But, look, Jackson was not a dumb politician. Years later, as he ran for the presidency, he did not resist the Kentuck myth. Imagine the poster if he had—square-jawed, white haired general Jackson, front and center, creoles, blacks, Indians and pirates filling in the background. That poster would have been an inspiring image of America, but white males were the only voters.

Let's look at a more modern myth, another variation on the rugged individual. Some individual genius invents the best of the best whatever in a garage. Sound familiar, did you think Bill Gates? It's so American; wouldn't it be wonderful if it fit the poor, under-privileged, Horatio Alger success story? Of course it doesn't. Bill Gates was attending Harvard, benefiting from considerable advantages, before he took off and started following his passion for software. I'd sure like to believe he spent time in a garage, it's such a working man's sort of space. Are there many spare garages in Harvard Square?

For me, the fact that the myth and the man don't fit together at all neatly doesn't really take much away from someone I admire. It takes guts to leave a prestigious university and go out on one's own. Well, not exactly on his own; he had friends and early corporate backing. He became one canny businessman and, after succeeding, one of the most decent philanthropists we have produced. But, his life story is instructive in that it deviates from the myth at crucial points. He is not a poor man making good on his own; he's a middle class, or even upper-middle class, man making good with help. And, what about Mark Zuckerberg (of more recent Facebook fame and riches)? He's also from Harvard, also backed by middle to upper middle class parents and friends.

Could it be that our future depends, at least in part, on encouraging such people? If so, then it would help to have a vibrant middle class reaching toward the upper middle class. Instead of encouraging that middle class, however; since Reagan, we have been busily gutting it. What's really disturbing, however, is that we continue to believe the middle class is doing way better than it is. We cling to the myth of a middle class while it disappears. Some of us even resent that portion of the middle class that manages to survive; policemen, firemen, teachers, and government workers, many still getting decent salaries and benefits. Right wing Republicans and Tea Party supporters target them as indiscriminatingly as our NJ Governor Christie. If I'm right about the real source of good old American creativity, gutting the middle class is the best way to make sure their children never become future Microsoft or Facebook game changers.

Here are the results of a study listing wealth by class.[11] The study includes the actual distribution of wealth among 5 levels of wealth as opposed to what we think the distribution is followed by several takes on what we would like to see as a fair wealth distribution.

Wealth—% of US assets owned (monetary as well as possessions) minus liabilities

Top 20%—Rich	85%
2nd 20%—upper middle class	11%
3d 20%—middle class	4%
4th & 5th 40%—lower class and poor	0.3%

That's how it is, or close, I've seen similar figures elsewhere.

Here's what the American public believes, according to one survey.

Rich	58% (not 85%)
Middle class	13% (not 4%)
Lower class and poor	9% (not 0.3%)

---

[11] Bruce Watson, 'Do Most Americans Favor Radical Wealth Distribution', "Daily Finance" posted 10/24/10

Interestingly, when dealing with figures, Americans, even the rich, tend to lean toward wanting a distribution of wealth closer to the much more equal one Swedish citizens enjoy. Does that mean we are all closet bleeding hearts, not rugged individualists? Nah—we're probably just confused, or maybe we have some instincts that favor fairness. Maybe we could go so far as to call these instincts social.

The last couple of national elections reflect some sort of confusion. The middle class center of the country, the rust belt that is in the most serious middle class decline, swung widely from supporting Obama in 2008 to rejecting him and his Democrat allies in 2010. The best explanation would seem to be that they are desperately casting about for solutions to their demise in terms of wealth and jobs without any firm notion of which solutions might work. They are pulled by starkly contrasting options. Fiscal stimulus advocates like Paul Krugman and more recently Ben Bernanke support more government action in the form of stimulus packages; deficit hawks want the government to balance the budget and then 'get out of the way'. Politicians thrive on confusion and starkly contrasting options. Blizzards of misinformation sound about as plausible as facts, dialogue becomes a shouting match. The result is seldom the right policy, certainly not a nuanced policy appropriate for complex problems.

After the recent election, I'm even less optimistic about the near term future of the country and particularly the middle class than I was several months ago. I see a number of scenarios playing out over the next two years, the worst much more likely than the better. Here's what I see as likely paths and outcomes:

1. Likely—Budget hawks (swept into office on the notion of less government and lowered taxes, even for those who have no need of extra money,) continue to support Bushonomics despite the evidence of the Bush years. They constrict government spending in the short term and then refuse to confront the long term deficit. Republicans were elected in 2010 based on the Bush eco-

nomic platform, and they weren't pressed by the public on long term deficits. They won once without a sensible plan that didn't work, why wouldn't they stick with a winning strategy, despite all their talk that this time they will act on their principles? We end up with both short term and long term failure.

2. Maybe—the presidential commission, reporting in December on the real long term deficit issues, provides enough cover so that both parties muster the courage to seriously address the long term deficit, but they fail to provide the stimulus and vision to address serious short and long term economic viability. Our infrastructure falls into further disrepair and we fail to prepare for the global competition of the 21st Century.

3. Real long shot—we, as citizens, actually see the present and the future for what it is and will be. Our politicians spend now, as they should, providing middle class construction jobs and building a 21st century infrastructure in order to help American businesses compete in the global economy. The middle class gains enough money building our future to begin spending and driving demand here in the US as they would, if they were working. Our products sell to the even more potent, future drivers of demand, the rising economic powers of Asia and South America. Businesses respond as they do to demand; they hire and expand. They are sitting on all the cash they need just waiting for demand. Our president and secretary of state actually succeed in their recent attempts to improve our trading positions with the rising economies. We make adjustments to Social Security, Medicare, Medicaid, and our military (the real deficit problems) from a position of economic strength, after we recover.

The right choice requires that we revise myths that do us harm. We don't do away with our faith in the rugged individualist; instead, we recognize that these days she or he is likely to be a well educated product of middle class or upper middle class parents with friends and with the guts to do something different. Further, we begin to allow ourselves to admit that we are not alone in the world. The well being of our fellow citizens not only matters it is critical to our economic survival, and so is the rest of the world. We need to confront problems as a more coherent society, and, eventually we need to recognize that doing so requires a high level of coordinated action.

Our passion for pretending that a smaller government is somehow a solution to ever more complicated, global issues seems like some sort of hangover from our mythic disdain for cohesive social action. We really do need to revive those instincts toward the socially cohesive units that actually won the west. Someone needs to inspire us with a counter myth or at least a myth that somehow merges the dream of the rugged individualist with something that could be seen as the nobility of collective action. Maybe we could just chuck the wagon train scenario and substitute movies about the greatest of 19th century social networks—the Underground Railroad. There were plenty of exciting tales, plenty of heroes, but the point was the network of cooperating human beings black and white, doing the decent thing out of heart-felt conviction. Couldn't we believe in that?

Hard Right

August 15, 2011

I am making an effort to understand the right wing of the Republican Party these days. They seem like a scattered collection of folks who are angry at this or that, a twitteresque collection of resentments; hard to find any consistency that I can think about in any coordinated way.

They seem to resent any interference from government in their personal lives and yet do not shrink from interfering in the relationship between women and their doctors or in the lives of homosexuals and lesbians. They espouse family values and yet show no mercy to illegal immigrant families. They complain vigorously about the dangers of the Mexican border, focusing entirely on border security, and yet they bristle at the least of attempts to control the automatic weapon purchases that make the border so dangerously insecure. They chant "kill the government beast" and "don't mess with my Medicare".

Economics would seem to be about the only area where this angry and vocal minority has something resembling a coordinated world view. Paul Ryan gave me a key to entering the economic world of the right wing when he revealed to the press that he had every member of his staff read Ayn Rand. Ah, I said, I must dip into Ayn Rand again (did I ever before?) to understand.

So, I Kindled up <u>Atlas Shrugged</u> and dug in with what enthusiasm I could muster. Before you heap too much praise on me for the nobility of my effort, I should mention that I've become bogged down on page 75, only 8% into the 1069 pages, as the nagging Kindle statisticians are far too anxious to inform me. It's enough, though, to get a sense of some broad character outlines as they are introduced and enough even to note an initial variation or two.

Dagny Taggart, daughter of Taggart Railroad's founder, is the clear (overly obvious) heroine—an intelligent, decisive, free spirit, willing to take risks and willing to accept consequences. Jim Taggart, her brother, is not too bright, he's indecisive or wrong-headed, easily misled and deceived, unwilling to take risks when he perceives risk and entirely unwilling to accept consequences.

Jim's a corporate man, president of the company because he's male and Dagny isn't. He has a mistress he abuses, and he takes credit for successful actions that are entirely his sister's doing. He has a certain loyalty to old business allies who fail to deliver, but worst of all, he sometimes confuses business with what borders on a perhaps less than sincere awareness of social issues.

Not too subtle so far, but there's a couple of other characters—variations on the theme. In many ways Francisco d'Anconia, a Mexican businessman, is the type of energetic entrepreneur Dagny admires. There are even hints of a past personal relationship. He has drive, he takes risks, he has massive influence, and he doesn't fail. And yet, something is wrong with the pitch he makes to Taggart Railroad and other potential investors. Dagny senses the problem and reacts sensibly; Jim falls for him and invests foolishly. Subtle plotting and subtle characters must come in the next 900 pages.

With Rupert Murdock in the news these days, I can't help seeing parallels with Ayn Rand's Francisco. Murdock's brilliant, he has the drive, he has influence, he takes risks, and he built an empire, just like Francisco. And, if it turns out he knew what was going on in his own company, he lacks any moral compass whatsoever, just like Francisco. So, for me, the question becomes—what moral compass keeps Dagny, who admires almost all of Francisco's Murdock like qualities, from becoming just another Francisco?

Wouldn't you know, Ayn Rand goes right on plotting answers to my obvious questions. I had to read a few more pages to see how it would work out. It seems that all the major railroad companies have developed an industry organization designed to promote railroads. We'd call it a lobbying group these days and in fact it acts like an industry organization worried about whether politics might work against industry interests.

Like such organizations today, when they see the threat of government regulation building, the railroad organization takes pre-emptive action by agreeing to their own self regulation. For the good of the country (you understand), they agree to an end of dog eat dog competition along major routes. The country's resources are not to be wasted building competing systems; it's just too crucial to move merchandise or raw materials along so many important routes to allow competition to siphon off railroad building capacity competing for a few prize routes. The parallel with recent government rulings regulating power transmission lines from the solar and wind rich areas of the southwest to the high electric power demand coastal areas is striking.

None of the railroad executives at the meeting really like the thought of regulating dog eat dog style combat (they're dog eat dog types at heart), but they pass the motion anyway. Jim Taggart wastes no time extolling the new agreement to Dagny because it eliminates Taggart's only competitor along the crucial Colorado line. The agreement stipulates that the older line on any route (Taggart for the Colorado route) gets the right to remain, and the newer (and in this case more efficient line) loses.

Even though Taggart Railroad wins, Dagny is incensed. The value she holds most dear, fair competition, has been violated. It's clear that none of the pious arguments about the good of the country have any meaning to her or to any of the railroad executives who mouthed them. She hurries off to visit the losing executive to find out why he acquiesced without more of a fight. She assures him that she would have fought him every way she could in a fair competition but to win this way was disgraceful.

So far the values are clear. She respects those who battle and win fairly. She does not like any regulation that might distort the free exercise of talent for any reason or from any source, not from industry organizations and certainly not from government. Add a corollary—nobody who doesn't strike out on their own with vision and determination really matters—and you have Randianism as I understand it so far.

Ayn Rand saves her best writing to fill out the differences between those who have the entrepreneurial talent and everyone else. The scene takes place in an underground, railroad terminal of enormous size. It's a New York City scene with people running this way and that way. Dagny is talking to a newspaper vendor who happens to have failed as an entrepreneur because his particular passionate interest didn't suit the times. Dagny likes him for his passion, even though he failed, and she sees what he sees. His description of the change in the terminal crowds is worth reading:

"I don't know. But I've watched them here for twenty years and I've seen the change. They used to rush through here, and it was wonderful to watch, it was the hurry of men who knew where they were going and were eager to get there. Now they're hurrying because they are afraid. It's not a purpose that drives them, it's fear. They're not going anywhere, they're escaping. And I don't think they know what it is that they want to escape. They don't look at one another. They jerk when brushed against. They smile too much, but it's an ugly kind of smiling: it's not joy, it's pleading. I don't know what it is that's happening to the world." [12]

One has to wonder what will become of these fearful people in the Ayn Randian world Paul Ryan admires so much. Such a stark contrast between the few remaining bold entrepreneurs and the many scurrying in fear leaves one with answers equally stark. I think I would not be completely unfair to cast subtlety aside (as Ayn Rand has up to this point in Atlas Shrugged) and give my own wide angle view of the Randian/Paul Ryan vision of the future. If I manage to push on further into Atlas Shrugged or even finish the

---

[12] Rand, Ayn (2005). Atlas Shrugged: (Centennial Edition) (p. 64). Plume, Kindle Edition.

monster, as I should, I can always follow up this entry with whatever appropriate revisions occur to me.

So, if we project the Ayn Rand world (as I see it so far) into the future, there will be a very small number of winners and a very large number of others. The others will include anyone who for any reason does not have the capacity to create and perhaps recreate themselves as economic demand shifts. Even those who build an empire one day may see it collapse the next in a Borders-like disaster if they are not quick enough to adapt. The others will certainly include anyone with diminished mental capacity. I'm thinking of very young children in the world's failed states with brains starved of critical early nutrition and/or early education or of the chronically left behind for whatever reason.

In today's world I doubt that the few winners by Ayn Rand standards could rise to more than 1 or 2% of the world's population. After-all this is not the halcyon age she looks back to in the section quoted above where men and women of energy could strike out into a USA of unlimited resources and build whatever they could dream. We now know, or should know, that with few exceptions everything we build damages something else. Build a pipeline, risk damaging a river. Build a development in the Pinelands, risk the Pineland ecosystem. The need to balance the effects of an entrepreneur's dreams against the public good is far more obvious now than in Ayn Rand's time.

Note, Paul Ryan, there is a public good to consider these days. And public good issues are not only the obvious—limited natural resources, exploding populations, and environmental degradation. There's the 98 to 99% of others Ayn Randianism does not cover, at least so far. I'm wondering what she will do with them as I push on through the rest of her opus.

But more important is what do the Paul Ryan's of the world propose doing with them? We used to talk about a race to the bottom. In a global economy the jobs generated by the entrepreneurial class go to those willing to suffer the most wherever they live. It makes business sense to make products where labor is cheapest. Slave labor is cheap and prevalent; so is child labor. No wonder they are both on the increase.

Of course the race to the bottom is not the only factor. Detroit, the symbol of expensive labor, is now making small cars again. Labor took a 50% cut in wages and cuts in benefits. The now successful Detroit plant became a poster child for robot labor meaning fewer workers with different talents. The hired workers will get by and the deal is good for them. But, the rub is that there are a lot fewer of them and a lot more robots. Are we talking about a USA with chronic human unemployment?

I listened to a Charlie Rose interview today with the CEO of Ford. To my surprise the CEO strongly advocated government/industry cooperation in building the infrastructure necessary to support the cars of the future. Investment in infrastructure requirements such as natural gas stations, electricity supply centers, and transmission lines cannot be done without government money; industry simply cannot do it alone, according to Ford's CEO. I've got to ask Paul Ryan and other small government advocates, not to mention Ayn Rand, how does that notion fit into your philosophy?

In a Paul Ryan world, with government regulation minimized, with entrepreneurs unopposed, with dwindling job opportunities, I wonder what the future of a democracy might look like. What comes to mind is some sort of fortress-like existence for the few and subsistence living for the many. I think of gated communities as the apt symbol of life in Paul Ryan's US of A. The few live there protected by fences and guards; the many eke out a living tending to the needs of the few. Hotel maids cater to their needs when they leave their fortresses.

It's hard to believe that a real democracy could survive. With money concentrated at the extreme top, how could democracy survive in anything but name only? Why I can even imagine the symbolic agent of the few, the corporation, becoming a super citizen with the immense political influence only money can provide. Does Paul Ryan's vision actually include support for the recent Supreme Court ruling that gave corporations the right to speak in our democracy as if they were individual citizens? I'll have to find out.

Finally, I see worship of the 'few' simply because they are among the 'few'. News outlets follow celebrities because they are celebrities, not because they have extraordinary talent. The 'others' will need diversion from their own subsistence existence, and these faux celebrities will cater to that need. I call this societal illness the Paris Hilton syndrome. Even the truly talented are tainted by it, having to suffer the fawning needs of others. A healthy society would admire talent and celebrate those who possess that talent. An unhealthy society grovels at their feet. I'll leave it to you to decide where we are likely to fall in the society the likes of Paul Ryan seem to envision. I'm far from charmed by it.

I will have to continue with another blog entry after I finish <u>Atlas Shrugged</u>. Last night in a fit of insomnia I came downstairs and read another 4%. The Francisco story line has become much more interesting with twists I didn't expect and don't fully understand.

Note: As of November, 2011 I have managed to reach page 863, 81% according to Kindle. I still hope for some indication that the Ayn Rand world is not as dire as I describe. There are threads that might come together at the end to brighten the outlook. January 17, 2012: During the final editing for this book, I pushed on to the culminating statement of Rand's philosophy as expressed by John Galt, the prime mover behind the destruction of the evil society built on need rather than ability. I doubt we will see many Republican politicians, who like Paul Ryan celebrate Rand's economics, tout Rand's view of religion, as expressed by John Galt. Religion and Socialism are linked as the two traditional enemies of the ideal reasonable man Galt (and Rand) advocate.

As Galt lectures, "For centuries the battle of morality was fought between those who claimed that your life belongs to God and those who claimed that it belongs to your neighbors–between those who preached that the good is self-sacrifice for the sake of ghosts in heaven and those who preached that the good is self-sacrifice for the sake of incompetents on earth. And no one came to say that your life belongs to you and that the good is to live it."

Rand, Ayn(2005-04-21). Atlas Shrugged: (Centennial Edition) (p. 926). Plume Kindle Edition.

CHAPTER 2
Democracy or Either/Or

Introduction

November, 2011

Democracy requires active citizens who take some time to think through issues. Even though we are a representative democracy, most of us would agree that leaving all the hard thinking and hard decisions entirely in the hands of our elected representatives would be unwise and, in fact, counter to what the founding fathers intended. Certainly they expected an informed citizenry, ready, willing and able to intelligently shape the opinions and policies adopted by their representatives.

And yet, so much works against the development of such a citizenry these days. Most of us scarcely have the spare time to glance at the headlines or skim through the first page of a newspaper. We are very likely to miss whole, 2 minute segments on the TV news channels because something comes up just before we reach the ads. Sorting through the internet clutter for reliable information without suffering from information overload is no quick and easy fix either.

If we aren't careful we end up accepting any source that makes a complex world seem simple. Easy choices, digested quickly become the fast fix, citizen's diet of the day. Bumper stickers and news opinion shows (more brawls than debates) entertain us rather than inform us. Our representatives are reduced to single categories— liberal or conservative, socialist or evangelical. The either/or choices hyped by the media and too often by our representatives often don't even conform to the simplest sense of what an either/or choice ought to be.

We end up in danger of becoming a twitter democracy, about as far from an informed, representative democracy as I can imagine.

Just before May 13, 2009, the date of the first entry in this chapter, the toast of a conservative convention was a 14 year old boy. I'm sure he was charming; but, in terms of constructing a sustained argument, I wouldn't expect him to get much beyond a tweet, about what I'd expect from a well trained parrot.

Liberal Conservative

Or a Liberal by Slight of Definition Makes His Claim to the Conservative Title—Why Not, Everyone Else Is Doing It

May 13, 2009

One of my friends willing to engage in political discussions via email (how old fashioned) recently described himself as a liberal conservative, meaning that in terms of social issues he was liberal but fiscally he was conservative. I've struggled in the past with the same sense of this split, but these days it's harder to figure out how one person can manage both inclinations at once. Saving the banking system and making progress on a number of long ignored but critical issues will cost whopping amounts of money up front, forcing those of us who would like to think we are still able to fence-sit to make some choices. Right now I'm clearly willing to relax fiscal conservatism in order to save the banking system and to make some progress on universal medical insurance, global warming, energy sustainability, infrastructure, and education; but I can understand the anguish of those who are not so willing, or who are at least nervous. I'm nervous.

So as not to lose all claims to a conservative strain, I've churned up some old thoughts about what the term conservative actually might mean. I've never liked most of the currently popular definitions; they sound like single notes on an overused, discordant instrument of some sort rather than like a finely tuned concerto; what one would expect from those who might wish to make a real claim to such an august title as conservative. To stretch the metaphor way too far, I'd like to suggest that we consider orchestrating a new, more harmonious definition, with complexity enough to be worthy of such a long admired concept.

Conservatism is not just a distrust of government, not just a 'lassie faire' economic theory, or just an attempt to define and practice a set of 'traditional' values. To think so is to reduce a complex human instinct to a plethora of Rush Limbaugh inspired, bumper sticker twitterisms. Conservatism should be something more fundamental from which these more popular positions derive, or perhaps from which these more popular positions make no sense at all.

We could start with Allan Bloom's[13] insistence that lacking an understanding of the great literary and philosophical works of the past we can hardly expect to envision a future that isn't tied to the whims of the moment. Most conservatives would agree, as would I.

Or, we could begin with a fundamental Christian tenant that mankind is beset by numerous moral weaknesses and therefore in need of divine guidance. A reasonable corollary would be that any construct (political, philosophical, scientific), cobbled together by morally weak beings, should be considered highly suspect, and therefore, if pursued, that concept should be pursued with a high degree of caution followed by constant re-evaluation.

Some Christians, those who unfortunately tend to capture far too much media attention, might argue about fine points of doctrine that often sound like the medieval dissertations on how many angels can fit on the head of a pin, but Christians would not be Christians if they did not heartily agree that humans are weak creatures in need of redemption and, when they act, in need of a healthy level of skepticism; and I would be hard put to imagine a conservative who wouldn't share that skepticism. I would share the skepticism, too, if not exactly the Christian reasons for it.

---

[13] The Closing of the American Mind

Or, we could begin our definition of conservatism with a merging of these two traditions, as the founding fathers did. Most of them were humanists[14] with classical educations; they constituted an intelligentsia Allen Bloom would applaud, but they didn't question such basic Christian tenants as the fallibility of mankind and, by extension, the fallibility of human institutions. That's why they established a finely tuned system (some might say an obsessive system) of checks and balances so that no one opinion or source of power could dominate. They built that balance into the legislative branch by attempting to place those they considered the wiser citizens in the Senate with longer terms to encourage longer views and then creating a more popularly based House with shorter terms so that the more immediate concerns of the general public could be represented, too.[15]

They checked both houses by providing for an independent executive with a veto power and then to counter-check the executive they provided a congressional override. They balanced the rights of the states against the powers of the federal government. They carefully circumscribed those federal governmental powers; then, just to be sure, they eventually agreed to a very specific Bill of Rights, just in case anyone ended up misinterpreting the scope of the original federal powers. They established an independent judiciary, in order to further ensure both the original rights and those specified in the bill of rights. One might reasonably describe the founders as conservatives, as I do; and the constitution they created usually meets with conservative approval. Of course they had just completed a rebellion against the preceding legitimate authority, so they were rebels, too.

---

[14] From what can be surmised, about 10% or so of the founder's generation considered themselves regular church-goers. They were more humanists than practicing Christians, more scientists than traditionalists. America went Christian big time (or you might say big tent time) in the mid 19th century. After the great awakenings of the 19th century, up to 80% of Americans considered themselves regular church-goers. Percentages were taken from Sean Wilentz, The Rise of American Democracy

[15] A more hard headed view of the founding fathers' purpose would include the need to encourage smaller states to sign on by giving them more power in the senate than they would have in the population based house. Politics as usual, a skeptic might say.

Wherever we start to define conservatism, the basics are clear enough. We simply cannot depend too heavily on the innate honor of individual humans to guide our affairs. Dictators or unbridled executives are simply not 'American', let alone conservative. We need conflict—clashing views and clashing sources of power, evenly balanced, as the founding fathers intended. If balance is what true conservatives should seek, then we could end up looking at some of the current, more extreme, neo-conservative calls for smaller government, 'lassie faire' economics, and even narrowly defined 'traditional values' as swings to one side, not conservative balancing but in some cases radical distortions, in other cases simply attempts to preserve comfortable distinctions.

Smaller government, for instance, does not mean very often that we are somehow freer, that power over our lives just disappears; more often it means that some other source of power dominates. We have a striking example of just where the power goes when we look into the sources of our current economic disaster. The Reagan revolution chipped away at government regulatory authority until there was too little regulation to balance the kind of creative greed likely to surface when manipulating other peoples' money. The power swung to the deregulated banks.[16] With no counter-balancing force, no alternate center of authority (like the government, for instance), some very large bank-like institutions stacked the cards all in their favor. They paid rating authorities[17] like Standard and Poor's to rate absurdly optimistic debt as

---

[16] Incidentally, we've experienced an even more down and dirty struggle between banks and the government before in our history. I'm in the midst of reading up on the conflict between Nicholas Biddle (banker early to mid 1800's) vs. the Federal Government and in particular Andrew Jackson (political transformer of the age). I'm not disappointed when government wins over bankers as Jackson finally did, sort of. At least I can vote for or against those who control government; I have no say over who runs banks.

[17] Food regulation suffers from the same compromised oversight. Food companies hire private inspectors to check their suppliers, which could work. The problem is that the private inspection company may have their inspectors both inspecting and selling the inspection service to the suppliers. There are cases where the same person

AAA, creating a Ponzi[18] scheme that makes Bernie Madoff's efforts look miniscule. Greed is not always good, despite a radically conservative mantra to that effect.[19]

The 'lassie faire' economic model that provides the rationale for smaller government seems to me to be limping along by relying on what has become an increasingly obvious flaw in the basic economic concept of value. I've harped on this before, but just to summarize, 'value' is no longer the sum of the value of the work and material that goes into creating something, or more simply, what the eventual user of a produced object is willing to pay for that work and material[20]. The production of objects has consequences beyond those that fit this narrow model—environmental, social, and moral consequences. It's high time for real conservatives to re-evaluate with those additional costs in mind. If they can come up with a way to add the cost of carbon creation, the collateral costs of resource depletion, pollution, slavery[21], poverty, revolution, terrorism, etc., into the value of produced goods without extending the influence of government, let's hear from them.

---

does both. When you are selling something it pays to make the buyer happy. Even I know that. Read, sure your peanuts are fine. Source (except for the tone of the peanut comment), NY Times article 3/6/09.

[18] A real ponzi scheme actually takes in money and then uses that money to pay off previous investors; no investment needs to take place. It works as long as there are enough new investors to cover withdrawals. What the banks and rating agencies did was not that crude. They took in money and paid off investors based on a wildly irresponsible assumption bordering on a con, that housing prices would go up forever. They had ½ a trillion worth of risk and an emergency fund of a few million. Like a Ponzi scheme, it worked until too many people wanted to cash in at once.

[19] Always puzzled me that neo-conservative economists can trumpet the virtues of greed as a stimulus to creativity and then turn to Christians for political support. Christians should at least recall the magnificent seven—lust, gluttony, **greed**, sloth, wrath, envy and pride.

[20] See Milton Friedman's pencil example of production and value recounted in Chapter 3 under entry 'Friedman 101'.

[21] Another hobby-horse of mine. I'm not going to forget that Tom Delay labeled, as an admirable example of free enterprise, the slavery still practiced under the American flag flying over the Mariana Islands. None of us should forget it. It's embarrassing to think that I'm waiting for our president to do something about this disgrace too.

All I can say to those conservatives who believe in the preservation of traditional values is that some so called traditional values have a way of evolving over time. I can't think of a founding father who didn't believe that citizenship should be firmly tied to property ownership. They felt that a citizen could not possibly act responsibly without that basic stake in the society and its government. White males with property voted; no one else. Of those criteria for responsible voters, property went first, male second, and finally white. Each change took time. These changes encountered vigorous, even murderous opposition, as attacks on 'traditional' values, but change happened anyway. I would venture to say that for most of the values neo-conservatives hawk these days, the pace of the change is the only real question. If they want to cling to values that will last, they really ought to consider returning to a traditional value that has lasted, human susceptibility to the seven deadly sins, for instance. I think I could go along with that.

The Chicken or the Egg?

July 30, 2010

You have no doubt all heard the startling news that science has finally given us a definitive answer to which came first—the chicken or the egg. I must admit that I always favored the chicken, and so the result is gratifying on two levels—as a nation we should be able to put this debate behind us, and the side I favored won. Though the result may seem trivial, we may be able to derive some real benefit by looking at the nature of the question itself, perhaps seeing it as a near perfect either/or logical proposition. Given the propensity of politicians and pundits for setting up overly simple and illogical either/or choices, such an exercise is no idle matter.

I should emphasize that I am not formally trained in logic; and, if I ever did receive any such training at all, over the last 40 or 50 years, I've certainly forgotten anything I might have learned, so I'm winging it here.

First, either/or has to be a choice. No fair picking both or even picking one and then later the other. It's the chicken and not the egg that came first, and that fact does not change when a chicken lays an egg producing a second chicken.

So far I think I haven't scrambled the logic of either/or. I'm not so sure about the next point, which I'll call proportionality. I would think that setting up a choice between seriously disproportionate options would render the choice a foregone conclusion, silly at best. You know that behind door A is 5 million dollars and behind door B is a nickel. I hope you don't need any help choosing; I don't, in case you were wondering. The only exception I can think of from my vast catalog of either/or choices proves the rule. If you were asked to choose which animal would frighten the other when they confronted each other, the elephant or the mouse, my niece informs me you'd be wrong picking the elephant. The mouse frightens the elephant, and it's a great story because it's so ludicrous. I'm sticking with proportionality as a requirement for serious either/or choices, though obviously you can set up any choice you want.

I've been working away on a third requirement, something to do with the result and the relationship between the result and the two options. I'm calling it interdependence; I might even insist on critical or clearly relevant interdependence. The chicken or the egg couldn't be more related in the sense I am hoping to convey. And the result has to be equally related to each option; in this case absolutely one or the other. I wouldn't require interdependence quite this tight in the real world, but the principle bares scrutiny anyway when evaluating the validity of less tightly constructed either/or choices.

I suppose at this point even my loyal reader(s) might wonder where I'm headed. It's one of the advantages of blogs that, unlike editorials, no one tells you where to start or when to end. I've been irritated recently by a massively inaccurate either/or choice sloppily put before the nation's citizens by simplistic politicians, lazy pundits, and thoughtless press sources. We are asked to believe that either we provide economic stimulus or address the budget deficit. I'd argue that this either/or fails all three of my logical validity tests, and yet Republicans, primarily, insist on arguing its validity over and over again, and even some Democrats seem seduced by its simplicity.

So, is either providing economic stimulus or reducing the budget deficit a true either/or choice where if you chose one you can't chose the other? Not at all. There is no reason why we can't provide short-term stimulus during an economic crisis and later reduce the longer-term deficit, once the economy recovers. In fact that's the Keynesian position. Those who insist on seeing short-term stimulus and deficit reduction as an either/or choice need to assume that once the stimulus starts it won't end and it won't morph into restraint later. A few who mouth the simpler either/ or construct even get this far in the argument. Actually they need to go a step further by denying or skirting around the possibility that the stimulus works, provides jobs, increases overall spending, improves the economy, raises the tax base, and therefore helps reduce the long-term deficit.

Perhaps we might agree to improve the either/or choice by restating it as follows—either reduce the deficit now by cutting spending, including any more stimulus spending, or stimulate now, allow the economy to recover, and then reduce the deficit; that's probably closer to a fair statement of the disagreement at this point. Note that choosing cutting spending now over stimulus now is a likely winner, if the recovery doesn't occur any time soon. By attacking any attempt at further stimulus those who insist on cutting spending now improve their odds—even unemployment extensions or aid to states has to go in order to give their side the best chance. Their Chicken Little hysteria about the deficit makes small business owners nervous about the future, adding yet another disincentive to expansion now, which is not what the economy needs now.

Either economic stimulus or deficit reduction fails the either/ or proportionality test too. The total stimulus bill that passed amounted to a one-time amount of $787 billion; so far $425 billion has been allocated. Compare that amount to the total military budget both base and wartime expenses of $782 billion in 2009, $855 billion in 2010, and a projected $895 billion in 2011. That means we are spending every year on the military alone more than a one-time stimulus designed to cushion the shock of a severe recession and perhaps depression. Here's the 2011 projections for a few other little spending items—Social Security, $730 billion; Medicare and Medicaid, $788 billion; other discretionary spending, $520 billion. To reduce the deficit, these are the yearly bills that are proportionally overwhelming, not the one time $787 billion stimulus package, even if you add in suggested extensions. It's the mouse and the elephant all over again, except this time it's the elephant in the room that will crush us. There is quite simply no sense in comparing the two in terms of proportionality.

Do the two choices have any relevant interdependence? Well, yes they do, sort of. Both can be related to the deficit. There is at least room to argue that the stimulus, plus any extensions to it, increase the deficit and therefore present a logical opposite to decreasing the deficit. To hold that position, as I've noted, requires ignoring Keynesian evidence to the contrary, but at least ignoring such evidence doesn't violate my interdependence rule. However, the two options do border on violating this rule if we look a bit more closely at the one-time vs. yearly distinction noted above under proportionality. A one-time expense, even with a few extensions, has an end point. All the real deficit generators do not. We will maintain a military. We are committed to paying retirees their social security checks. Medicare and Medicaid will continue. In fact, US demographics almost insure that two of the major deficit generators, Social Security and Medicare will increase as the population ages, even if we take steps now to reduce them.[22]

---

[22] A better either/or in terms of relevant interdependence might be which stimulus works—either the Bush high-end tax cuts defended as a trickle down stimulus or the Obama more direct government stimulus. Both Paul Krugman and the conservative Heritage Foundation see the Bush tax cuts as reducing revenue from their inception to 2009 by $1.8 trillion, more than twice the Obama stimulus amount. The Heritage Foundation goes on to argue that 25% of that was recovered through what they claim was a stimulative effect, bringing the revenue decline down to $1.34 trillion($1.8 trillion-25% of $1.8 trillion), still significantly more than the Obama stimulus. Krugman would argue that the tax cut stimulus effect was temporary at best and did not trickle down. And, we ended up with a deficit followed by a crash. Let's hope we kill those high-end tax cuts for good. Estimates for 2009-2018, if we don't kill them, would amount to $4.4 trillion.

I asked my congressman today (July 23, 2010), at a town meeting, why he didn't support a $30 billion House bill to stimulate small business expansion and resulting job creation. The House bill provides low cost capital to small banks if they in turn provide loans to small businesses. It encourages private equity investment in startups and small businesses by pairing SBA funds with private investments, among other

The debate we should be having about the deficit has almost nothing to do with the stimulus. We should be pressing our representatives with real questions about military strategy, social security adjustments, and Medicare/Medicaid cost rather than allowing them to divert our attention with false choices.

An odd combination of political players made a start recently when Barney Frank and Ron Paul seemed to agree that any real discussion of military spending needed to begin with a review of our strategic objectives. Is there some reason why we continue to consider ourselves as the number one NATO military provider? Say, maybe Germany, France, or Britain could take over the lead. Do we really need a base in Japan? Maybe we could keep a base on the Mariana Islands, or maybe Japan, Australia, or the Philippines could pick up the slack if we pulled back a bit. We spend more on our military than all other countries combined. That's absurd, and we need to change it if we intend to seriously wrestle with the deficit. Picking away at waste and individual weapon systems won't do the job; a strategic rethink might.[23]

---

measures. The treasury would receive dividend paying preferred stock as collateral. He won't support $30 billion for direct stimulus but doesn't seem to flinch at $1.8 trillion for the directionless approach Republicans seem to want to continue to palm off on us, as I pointed out to him.

[23] Tea Party members might recall the following statement by a prominent Republican.

"We annually spend on military security more than the net income of all United States corporations.

This conjunction of an immense military establishment and a large arms industry is new in the American experience. The total influence — economic, political, even spiritual — is felt in every city, every State house, every office of the Federal government. We recognize the imperative need for this development. Yet we must not fail to comprehend its grave implications. Our toil, resources and livelihood are all involved; so is the very structure of our society.

In the councils of government, we must guard against the acquisition of unwarranted influence, whether sought or unsought, by the military/industrial complex. The potential for the disastrous rise of misplaced power exists and will persist.

We must never let the weight of this combination endanger our liberties or democratic processes. We should take nothing for granted. Only an alert and knowledgeable citizenry can compel the proper meshing of the huge industrial

The health bill contains a number of approaches to controlling medical costs. These costs are straining local and state government insurance budgets for employees as well as Medicare and Medicaid (federal and state). Any politician who opens his/her mouth about the deficit should immediately hear a question about what needs to be done about these costs. We simply cannot afford to let them get away with dodging these real budget questions any longer. Ask them if they supported options within the health bill that encouraged discussions between doctors and patients about living wills. If they didn't, they aren't serious about medical cost control, period. Did they support review of best medical practices? Did they support the public option? If not, ask them what medically related, deficit reduction measures they did support. Then ask them how much they think their measures might go toward deficit reduction.[24]

In December the report by the presidential committee to investigate solutions to the deficit is due. We might ask our representatives why congress didn't initiate this review, and we could start asking what solutions they hope to see in this report. We need to begin asking real questions; chicken or egg formulations are far too simple. Just a few suggestions I would hope to see in the report.

1. A complete review of our military strategy followed by an implementation plan. Let's aim at a figure around ½ what the rest of the world spends. The strategic review must include troop needs. The troops and their direct support, not weapons, are by far the greatest part of costs. Of course troop reductions

---

and military machinery of defense with our peaceful methods and goals, so that security and liberty may prosper together."
-Pres. Eisenhower, 1961.

[24] Republicans are fond of bringing up malpractice reform. I've gone into just how inadequate that particular proposal is in previous blog entries. See Chapter 6, 'Republican Healthcare Plan', February 1, 2010

mean we don't send our troops in every time a petty dictator acts like a petty dictator.

2. Social Security adjustments like those passed in 1983. People live longer so we need to adjust partial and full payment ages accordingly.

3. A slight increase in the payroll tax. This tax needs to reflect changes in the costs of the programs it supports and changes in demographics. Some of costs of the aging population could be offset by passing a sane, legal immigration policy. Immigrants tend to be young workers.

4. Permanent rejection of the Bush tax cuts. The income tax needs to go back to being much more progressive. If you want to support small business, there are much more direct ways to do that than giving all the rich a break. Think of it this way, many of the rich work on Wall Street, a few work for BP, a significant number inherited their wealth. Republicans in the Senate are busy killing a loan program for small businesses, incidentally, though they masquerade as small business supporters.

5. Serious consideration of the way we handle medical care compensation. As I've argued previously, paying for results beats paying for procedures. Paying doctors salaries, as large medical providers such as Kaiser Permanente do, relieves them of business related details and malpractice insurance expenses, allowing them to concentrate on medical results.

6. Take all subsidies for oil development and switch them to renewable energy subsidies. Add a carbon tax. We really need to get on with the 21st century before the real costs of carbon-based energy sink us. Real costs include the destruction of the Nigerian delta, the Gulf of Mexico disasters (past, current and ongoing), supporting some of the world's worst regimes and most irresponsible companies, bad air, bad water, and the loss of the Saugerties lighthouse.

7. Continue to press for repayment from those who received Troubled Asset Relief Program funds (TARP funds). This program,

started at the end of the Bush administration, incidentally, is showing signs of considerable success. Several large banks have paid back in full, plus interest; others are close. GM is considering a stock sale, which might well mean all or a good portion of that money will come back. And, GM is profitable again thanks to sales in China. China as a consumer—think of that, we don't have to buy everything any more, just to keep the world economy afloat. According to an AP article as of 6/22/10 TARP had distributed $205 billion of the $707 billion allocated and $142 billion has been repaid. AIG, Freddie Mac, and Fanny Mae are the worst of the lot. We need to address Fanny and Freddie, somehow. Check out the web to follow the amounts allocated to every recipient, the amounts they have returned, and the profits our government made on each transaction. Sample on the good side—Bank of America $45 billion allocated, $45 billion returned, $5 billion government revenue. Really bad—AIG $48 billion of the $70 billion committed already distributed, none returned, $0 revenue.

Political Ads? Forget About It

October 26, 2010

I've developed what I consider a solution to political advertising, a solution that any concerned citizen can implement this very day. We don't need to legislate in order to correct the distressing Supreme Court ruling that found some incomprehensible way to equate a corporation to a person in terms of first amendment rights[25]; we don't even need to know who financed a particular ad, though of course we have a right to know. All we need to do is look at any political ad with the following thoughts in mind. Political ads are either:

1. Out and out lies. Swift boat ads come to mind.
   Or:
2. Such over-simplifications of complex issues as to be useless to anyone who thinks. Take the death panel claims for example.
   Or:
3. Blatant or coded appeals to prejudice. Reagan's welfare queens, for example.
   Or:
4. Special interest attempts to buy influence. Just one example, recent ads put out by the Better Business Bureau. I used to rely on them for accurate information on the legitimacy of

---

[25] Whatever happened to those guys who started a corporation in order to see just how many citizen rights they could claim for a purely legal entity? Last I heard they were seeking to run their corporation for congress. Do corporations have freedom of religion too? Does that mean they have the right to exclude Christians, Muslims, Jews, etc.?

individual businesses. Maybe they still give out such information, but they have seriously tarnished their brand for me. Or:

5. Personal attacks. So many tend to come out at the last minute when they are particularly difficult for voters to verify.

Though, as a Democrat, examples of Republican ads seem to come readily to my mind, I do believe firmly that the above approach should be applied to Democratic ads too. Let's just consider ignoring all this misleading twaddle as our civic duty. Of course, if we do, then, as responsible citizens, we need to seek other sources for information about issues and candidates. Wouldn't you know, I have a number of rules to follow here, too.

1. Any news program that treats politics as a blood sport or some equally venal form of entertainment should be turned off. I followed my own advice recently by turning off an MSNBC program, despite its liberal bias.

2. Choose a television or radio station by how many minutes it devotes to a single topic. NPR and PBS actually spend significant amounts of time analyzing issues, as does the BBC. Sometimes even the networks like ABC have extensive coverage of specific issues extended over a number of broadcasts. We should encourage them.

3. Find an interview program where the person being interviewed gets a chance to speak more than one paragraph before being interrupted by the host. Charlie Rose comes close, though at times even he interrupts more than I would like. The point is that an interview should be about the person being interviewed, not the host.

4. Read newspapers that reach a 2nd page with an article and then use the whole 2nd page to finish. If an issue matters, it deserves a full explanation, not a headline followed by a blurb.

5. Read books. Sometimes issues deserve fuller development by someone who went to the trouble of spending oddles of time thinking. For current economic issues, try Milton Friedman followed by Paul Krugman.
6. Go to original sources. Example—if you are going to mention your reverence for the constitution, give a thought to reading it. Even better, read <u>Hamilton, Madison, and Jay, The Federalist with Letters of "Brutus"</u>. This Cambridge text cross references the Federalist papers and the anti-Federalist "Brutus" papers to the constitution and its amendments. Another example—read the candidates' actual web pages.[26]

Even when I follow my own advice, I find myself falling into traps set by my accustomed lines of thought. Recently our governor, here in New Jersey, decided to cancel a new mass transit tunnel under the Hudson, designed to significantly improve the capacity to transport people who live in NJ into NYC where many of them work. I've been hearing about this project for at least 20 years. I listen to auto traffic reports as I'm sipping my morning coffee, so I know that our neck of the woods (what woods you say) needs mass transit infrastructure improvements like few others.

The tunnel is needed infrastructure improvement; it would provide massive construction job increases; interest rates for financing it are low now; the federal government is finally trying very hard to give New Jersey something back on our disproportionate financial contributions to running the country, rather than sending the money to Alaska—how could our governor possibly be so stupid as to refuse? He argues that cost overrun estimates

---

[26] The web pages run from single sentence platitudes like those on Christine McDonald's to better reasoned, rehashed Reaganomics like Linda McMahon's to the Libertarian thoughts of Rand Paul. Voting records on all bills are readily available too, though reasons for particular votes can be difficult to sort out. Many votes are merely tactical, for example. I began this blog nearly 4 years ago by trying to evaluate the voting records of two local congressmen, one conservative and one liberal. Interesting to me at the time, but as you can see, I gave up.

are out of line, and that New Jersey would be forced to pick up any extra tab. That's just pennywise foolishness. Cost overruns occur, but the projected overruns in this case are not so out of line that they come anywhere near the cost of losing the project's long term benefits to New Jersey's productivity or the cost of losing construction jobs in the short term.

So, that was my initial take on the governor's move, and I might well have left that opinion intact, (since it fit so neatly into my general conception of Governor Christie) if I hadn't happened to read a New York Times letter to the editor that raised a completely new question about the project. The letter argued that the project was flawed because it did not terminate at the right point in the city. The letter writer stated that the planned terminus would benefit NJ Transit running from NJ to NYC and back but not transit running north. I did have a fuzzy notion of some controversy about which piece of NYC real estate would suffer from the project, but I had no idea that the controversy involved a functional issue. Too bad the writer didn't have space to elaborate. Too bad the Times didn't follow up with an article.

The thought that I might have missed something important about the tunnel project did cause me to reconsider the governor's moves. I looked for something to indicate that he knew of some tunnel design issue. If so he didn't make news by bringing it up forcefully enough. I heard nothing further from him on the design issue or from anyone else. I did begin to think that maybe the governor was playing some sort of high stakes poker with transportation secretary LaHood to gain even more advantages for New Jersey. He's extended the timetable for his decision; he seems to have induced the secretary to sweeten the pot; maybe he's not stupid but, in fact, tactically clever. We'll have to wait and see. Lesson learned once again: watch out when what you read fits too neatly into preconceptions. Think again and then wait a bit.

I'm going to give myself some credit here. I have never argued that God supports my view. I consider anyone who does as being beyond the pale, so arrogant about his/her own sense of what's right as to attribute their views to God. Yet, I fear, this sort of non-argument actually motivates people who vote. Here's some sample comments from a couple of folks who don't believe that global warming is a man made phenomena.

Indiana Tea party organizer Norman Denison—referring to global warming, said "It's a flat-out lie…I read my bible. He made this earth for us to utilize."

Lisa Deaton, another Indiana Tea Party organizer said "being a strong Christian I cannot help but believe the Lord placed a lot of minerals in our country and it's not there to destroy us."[27] The point here is that people who sink to arguing that they are right because they presume God supports their views should be dismissed without any further comment.

---

[27] New York Times article October 21, 2010

CHAPTER 3
Larger Government—Get Used to It

Introduction

November, 2011

I'd love to believe our population is getting smaller, our problems less complex, our relations with the rest of the world less intricate, and our environment less inter-connected, but I don't believe any of these notions are true. If I did, I might jump aboard the smaller government choo-choo. Instead I believe government will inevitably enlarge to meet larger more complex challenges.

Do we really need fewer employees at the Securities and Exchange Commission as banks that have now been allowed to become investment firms devise ever more ingenious ways to risk our economy? Do we need fewer federal inspections of the food supply as we hear almost weekly of yet another outbreak of food poisoning or as the sources of our food widen to ever more suspicious areas of the planet? Do we need fewer court employees as cases back up, fewer park rangers as our parks deteriorate—fewer oil rig inspectors, fewer fracking inspectors, and fewer folks at the FDA or NIH?

Despite what I see as needs requiring larger government, small government advocates seem to be enjoying a renaissance. They derive much of their logical underpinnings from conservative economic philosophy and in particular the works of Milton Friedman. So, I read Friedman in order to see what he might have been thinking. What I found surprised me and might well surprise today's small government advocates. There is plenty of room for government action in his economic theory. However, he does object strenuously to government interference in what he sees as an intricate and productive free enterprise system. It's that part of his theory today's conservatives cling to and that part I find seriously in need of a 21st century update.

This chapter on larger government connects so closely with the next chapter on our place in the world that I had difficulty deciding which blog entry belonged where. If there is any area where our government will need to enlarge it is in helping to bring the world together to solve international problems.

Energy Independence?
Nonsense

September 26, 2007

I sent the following to the NY Times 'Letters to the Editor' in response the Robert Cohen's op-ed piece in which he argued that how we leave Iraq is more important than how we got there.

How we exit Iraq is important, but not more important than how we got there, as Robert Cohen argues. He clarifies in the final paragraph stating that global stability hinges on the credibility of American power, which depends on how we leave Iraq. Certainly the credibility of our power plays a part short term; but we really need to discuss how to join the world in seeking long-term stability.

Long term, global stability will require Americans to think dependence, not independence. Independence comforts us, but serious problems—global warming, traveling viruses, lowering wages—require recognition of our interdependence.

On every front, from Kyoto to land mines, we need to join the world in establishing international norms leading to internationally enforced laws. Not learning this lesson from the Bush, 'go-it-alone' debacle means missing a critical opportunity to correct the neo-conservative misdirection that got us into Iraq.'

I've been struck recently by the term 'energy independence'. All of our current presidential candidates repeat the goal. Somehow corn based ethanol, wind power, solar power, natural gas, atomic energy, and energy conservation all get wrapped up in this US centric notion that we are somehow independent from the rest of the world's needs for the same commodities. Of course this is nonsense. We all know that how the rest of the world reacts to energy needs will have serious consequences for them and for us. What I'm waiting for is the candidate who consistently replaces the term energy independence with energy sustainability. Words matter, as I've argued ad nausea.

Once we switch to energy sustainability, it will be hard to ignore the rest of the world. We might even prefer Brazilian sugar cane produced ethanol to Iowa produced corn ethanol because it is so much more sustainable. Right now our government, as part of its energy independence policy, supports Iowa corn through farm subsidies by about the same amount as it taxes Brazilian imported ethanol. Watch for the politician willing to confront a farm lobby that certainly no longer needs support (corn is in short supply) and then drops the import taxes for Brazil. If such a political creature exists, we should back him/her. Of course, we'd be backing a loser, unless we all begin to realize what's at stake.

Questions for Democratic Presidential Candidates

December 2, 2007

Now that Mike Ferguson has joined many other Republican representatives by announcing that he will not run in 2008, tracking his voting record and comparing it with Rush Holt's, the original purpose of this blog, no longer seems quite so relevant. At some point I will try to finish up that project by noting and documenting what I think may be a somewhat recent shift from the right toward the center by Mr. Ferguson, partly for the sake of completeness, but mainly because I think that his change may mirror the general shift nationwide toward a more progressive role for government, so hopefully outlined by Paul Krugman in his latest book.

For now, though, I'll continue what I had somewhat unintentionally allowed to happen to this blog. It's become more my own general political commentary and less concerned with the local candidates. I will try to shift back to the views of local candidates on important national interests, once we know who those candidates will be.

In the back of my head, recently, I've been trying to formulate a question for the presidential candidates that would get them off their various hobbyhorses and reveal something about just how ready they are to govern in the 21st century. I guess I've been listening to too many questions from the moderators and the general public during the debates, questions that seem to play to the old worn out issues. The candidates all have their answers ready for those questions.

Unfortunately I can't seem to come up with a single question. In general I want to know if they are ready to face the real 21st century need to balance the power of global mega-corporations, with an equally powerful global legal presence, backed by international organizations capable of enforcement. In <u>Jihad vs. McWorld</u> Benjamin Barber (1995) describes the explosive and innovative expansion of now powerful global companies and the weak and ineffective response from our current international governing institutions. As he points out, the nation states can't really regulate internationally. And, we receive evidence that international organizations lack the power every time we hear about yet another affront to what most of us would consider basic values like no slavery, no child labor, and yes, the freedom to protest, organize, and move about freely.

As Benjamin Barber points out, these are values we established in the US and in other relatively progressive countries in opposition to the 19th and early to mid 20th century, industrial robber barons. It's that portion of our labor history we can be proud of, but it does not seem to be that part of the value system we are willing to help build into effective international law. Part of our hesitancy is simply isolationism. We don't want to give real power to organizations beyond our borders. We haven't even begun to address the issue of our sovereignty vs. the need for sovereign power globally. Europe has made a beginning by establishing the European Union, and we can see from their struggles what a long road it is to any effective governing body larger than nation states.

Other powerful forces work against reasonable regulation of global companies, too. The US in particular, but certainly not exclusively, has been infected by the neo-conservative notion, spread by would be followers of Milton Friedman, that unfettered capitalism will regulate itself. This 'greed is good' (because it sparks innovation) crowd makes a couple of fundamental mistakes. They overstate the connection between greed and innovation, excluding the possibility of other motivations. They ignore the possibility that the good might be accompanied by some bad. Their thought leads directly to atrocities like the industrial slavery of the Mariana Islands so lavishly praised as a fine example of free enterprise by the likes of Tom Delay and Jack Abramoff. How evangelical Christians, who should have read a thing or two about greed, could have accepted this economic creed as part of their far right coalition baffles me.

Opposing both isolationism and developing a global system of law and order to match the power, influence, and success of global mega-corporations, now that's a task for a leader I could support. I don't see anyone on the political spectrum standing up for an effective World Trade Organization. We need a WTO capable of correcting the excesses of corporations to replace the one we have now, dedicated as it is to supporting corporate reach. All we get, even from progressives, are largely unsuccessful attempts to build controls into regional trade agreements, and maybe that's all we can expect for now, but I hope not.

So, my question for the presidential candidates needs to press them toward support of truly global legal solutions while preventing them from taking the easy road by touting their trade agreement toughness. Here's a go at it—

Benjamin Barber in <u>Jihad vs. McWorld</u> describes the overwhelming power of today's global mega-corporations and decries the weakness of international legal organizations that might provide a needed corrective to their excesses. What would you do as president, beyond tweaking regional trade agreements, to support the development of effective international law necessary to counter the anti-worker and anti-environmental policies that too often result from the quite legitimate pursuit of the bottom line by successful global corporations?

I'll send the question out to as many candidates as possible and report results.

After sending emails to Hillary Clinton, Barack Obama and John Edwards, I changed the last part of the last sentence to read—… the anti-worker and anti-environmental policies that too often result from an over-zealous pursuit of the bottom line by successful global corporations.

Milton Friedman 101

January 10, 2008

With the primaries now headed from New Hampshire to Michigan, economic issues should take up more room on the front page than they have so far. The subject might even eclipse the TV time devoted to tears, smiles, and smirks. There are plenty of economic subjects to talk about—the bursting housing bubble, endless increases in oil prices, increases in the jobless rate, plummeting job creation, a seriously declining dollar, the global race for resources, our competitiveness up and down the economic scale, the tattered safety net, and maybe even consumption itself. If we are going to discuss economic issues seriously, though, rather than just repeating old mantras, we ought to start by chipping away at worthless labels like socialism or free trade, liberal or neo-conservative, when the terms are used as negatives. Political terms live far too long, outliving their usefulness, for sure, but worse, eventually obscuring facts and distorting the discussion to the point where what we hear becomes down-right harmful.

As anyone who knows me will quickly attest, I'm not without my own set of locked in economic/political notions. Knowing this myself, to some extent, I swallowed a touch of corrective medicine by reading the laissez-faire guru Milton Friedman, both <u>Money Madness</u> and <u>Free to Choose</u>. This is not delightful reading, more like castor oil, especially when he gets into what the Federal Reserve and banks actually do; but there are moments of real clarity, sort of like when a headache suddenly dissipates. I'd like to think that some of our politicians, especially those who use catch phrases from Friedman, have taken their medicine recently and read or reread him, but I have my doubts.

Very broadly put, one of the questions Friedman addresses is how far government should go in attempting to influence the operation of the free market. Interestingly enough the answer is not what many politicians and free market enthusiasts seem to think; Friedman does not advocate a complete lack of interference. He follows Adam Smith by pointing out that we are not free if our society is lawless or if another society attacks us and prevents our commerce. But both Friedman and Adam Smith add a third category for government action, public works—those necessary enterprises, which never could repay an individual or small group of individuals sufficiently for them to contemplate the enterprise in the first place. Think the federal highway system attributed to Dwight D. Eisenhower, a Republican, incidentally.

The argument really begins, as Friedman points out, with the third category. To update his examples, think Amtrak; for the most part we've stopped debating the advisability of a federal highway system, but a federal versus a private rail system, that's still a hot topic. Friedman goes on to what he describes as the problem of unintended consequences. When somebody's private business action has an unintended effect on someone else, smoke or pollution for instance, shouldn't the government step in to provide redress? As Friedman notes, it is difficult for an individual entrepreneur to evaluate the damage, and it's also difficult for the government to do so. And, when the government does step in, as Friedman is quick to point out, that action may well have unintended consequences of a detrimental nature too.

If you believe in individual entrepreneurial initiative and in effective government, as I do, the question of when the government should step in and when it should not requires us to consider possible interventions carefully, on an individual basis. Throwing the label socialist at anyone advocating government action, no matter what the issue, or neo-con at someone who opposes a particular government action, will not get us far in addressing each case. In fact the labels simply end the conversation and obscure creative solutions.

For each issue there's a scale that runs from those like Friedman, who tend toward extreme caution, more afraid of the unintended consequences than worried about the problem, to a Paul Krugman[28], who firmly believes government action has proven itself in the past and will again, once we shed the Bush administration and regain faith that government can work. Here's the deal. I'll try hard to stop calling the over cautious folks neo-cons (with a definite sneer on my face) if Kristol and Romney will drop socialism from their vocabulary. OK to call me a liberal; I consider that a compliment. In fact to get me on the scale, you would need to extend it on the government works side to include, as Benjamin Barber[29] does, (horror of horrors for the cautious folk) effective international government.

If we look at what is happening to the fundamental Friedman concept of price over the last few years, we'll see just how the scale can slide over time. Friedman (writing in 1980) had a strict definition of price; he saw price as critical to the functioning of a free market, entrepreneurial system. Price was the communication method from section to section of the immensely complex network required to produce anything. He describes what needs to happen in order to manufacture a pencil. Someone needs to produce wood and lead, someone needs to produce saws and other logging equipment, someone needs to produce fuel for the saws and logging equipment, and on and on.

None of these individual entrepreneurs or companies, except the pencil manufacturer, knows anything about the pencil business, but decisions made by any of them about what they do know, if significant enough, will make its way back to the pencil guy in the way of price changes. Suddenly cedar trees become scarce and thus higher in price, everyone wants cedar, pencils go up in price; then the pencil guy decides, well, some other wood will do, or maybe I'll invent something, ah-ha, mechanical pencils.

---

[28] Paul Krugman, The Conscience of a Liberal
[29] Benjamin Berger, Jihad vs. McWorld

Strict economic conservatives would say that interference with such an elaborate system simply distorts the information or adds noise to the communication and will in the end delay adaptation, reduce innovation, and generally lead to undesirable distortions of an elegant, naturally functioning system.

Unfortunately for elegant systems in general, they do not get to operate in the kind of isolated world elegance requires. For instance, just adjusting the price of cedar upward, while it signals changes accurately within the limited world of individual economic incentive, such a price change as defined by Friedman says nothing about the natural world that is affected as well. There is after-all a much more intricate, complex and natural system than economics, the environment, that we now understand responds to our economic decisions. It's odd to me that conservative economists, who show so much respect for restraint when fiddling with the delicate economic system, fail to show similar caution when dealing with the much more complex natural system.

Fortunately there are economists who do recognize that price needs to reflect effects other than those that are purely economic. In fact Friedman was one of them. We now hear lots of talk about cap and trade or carbon taxes. Conservatives should note that Friedman proposed carbon taxes as an incentive for industry to improve their environmental impact in <u>Free to Choose</u>. Almost thirty years later it's time to put such sensible proposals into law. Liberals and conservatives (who follow Friedman) should be able to agree on this simple change; even if such changes get rolled into the price we all pay.

It now seems fairly clear that we need to consider the cost to the environment, but there are other costs too. Strict price definitions say nothing about ending child labor, ending slavery, or other labor values that have become part of our moral fabric. Many are beginning to believe that we ought to price some level of moral responsibility into the cost of our consumption. Some would even go so far as to question the 'consumption at all costs' mentality itself that underlies Friedman economics.

Can government help make some of these price adjustments? I think sometimes yes and sometimes no. Government can pass cap and trade or carbon taxes now that leaders like Al Gore have done the groundwork. Government has outlawed domestic child labor and domestic slavery, but we don't have an international government to enforce even these basic labor concerns beyond our borders. Changing attitudes toward consumption? I have difficulty doing that myself, and I call myself progressive. I'll work on it though, and meanwhile I'm not interested in having governments help me along quite yet. Price, itself, is sliding along the scale toward a more inclusive definition. We'll see just how far we go in the next decade or so.

Friedman 102

January 27, 2008

I wanted to follow up my previous posting with some response to two specific areas of private vs. governmental action discussed in some detail by Milton Friedman in <u>Free to Choose</u>. He has chapters on education vouchers for private schools vs. public schools and on private vs. governmental medical insurance programs. In the case of schools he argues for the introduction of private vouchers and against the public school monopoly; in the case of medical care he supports the private status quo against the introduction of a government run insurance system. Much has happened in both areas since the 1980 publication date of <u>Free to Choose,</u> but the arguments he advanced still sound remarkably familiar.

Believing, as I do, in both private initiative and responsible government, I do not find the answers to these questions quite as cut and dry as Friedman based conservatives or some liberals do. I have been intrigued over the years by school vouchers and by the alternative schools they are designed to encourage. Long ago, after I'd taught college freshman for a number of years, my wife and I discussed starting a school. We didn't have any revolutionary ideas; we just wanted a place where students and their teachers could follow engaging projects over extended periods of time, working without textbooks and without narrowly defined subject disciplines. As it turned out, we had no money, no physical facility, and without voucher programs, little likelihood of finding students.

Vouchers and the notion of alternative schooling would have helped. I'm not at all opposed to either. Like many liberals, I do wonder what would happen to public schools if voucher pro-grams were wide spread. Would public schools become dump-ing grounds for hopeless students? Would wealthy families use vouchers to send their children to ever pricier, elite institutions? Would the vouchers simply expand the opportunities for those who could almost but not quite afford private school? Would the amount of money available for vouchers really be enough to reach down to those who have no alternatives without draining the pool of money available for public education? Friedman had answers to some of these questions (not all satisfactory), but even he admitted that realizing a fully effective voucher system seemed politically inconceivable.

He touched on other concerns too. Where would we draw the line in terms of what moral values got taught in voucher supported schools? Would we give vouchers to Catholic school students learning the catechism, fundamentalist school students learning biblical literalism, madrassa students learning Islam? If so, would we be helping to fragment the few threads of commonly held val-ues that hold us together as a nation? Friedman does not go very far into these questions, other than to note that public schools can't help but inculcate certain values, too, based loosely on the constitution and the humanist tradition behind it. I'd vote to limit education supported by public funds to the values enshrined in the constitution, whether supported by vouchers or by the meth-ods that currently predominate. Those who wish to teach other values remain perfectly free to do so on their own dime, as they do today, without vouchers.

As Friedman argued, at every opportunity, competition leads to innovation, monopolies to stagnation. So, why aren't those who are willing to try out public/private competition in education through a voucher system, willing to accept public/ private competition in the health insurance field? Currently we have reasonably effective public health insurance for seniors and military personnel, and we have private health insurance for the dwindling number of workers who receive it through company plans or who can afford it on their own. For the most part the systems do not overlap, so they don't in general compete. Only the recent private Medicare Advantage plans serve the same public (Medicare age seniors) as publicly financed Medicare, and they are privately run plans but subsidized by the government (up to 14%)—some sort of hybrid.

What we have, as a medical insurance system, is broken. It's more expensive than other systems, it's annoyingly complex, it delivers measurably poorer health results than European plans, and 47 million Americans and counting can't afford it or refuse to pay for it. Just as I don't object to private/public competition in education through a voucher program, I would not object to fair competition between public and private medical insurance models, across the board, if they competed on a fair playing field. The fair playing field underlies John Edwards' detailed health insurance plan, the first one offered by the presidential candidates, if you don't count Republican health savings accounts, (I don't). Fair means no subsidies by the government for private plans like the subsidies offered to Medicare Advantage plans. Fair means that private insurers do not get to cherry pick their clients and leave the sick and the poor to government plans.

If we believe in universal insurance, then both private and public plans need to offer the prospect of universality. Edwards and others specify that if insurance companies intend to operate in a particular area, then they must accept all applicants in that area, as the government does. I would think both government and private plans ought to provide some level of baseline coverage to all. Let the private market compete by offering better service, better preventive care, streamlined paper work, lower premiums, expanded coverage, supplemental coverage, provider networks, different donut holes, different deductibles, different co-pays, or whatever else they can think to offer beyond the basics. There would be plenty of room for innovation, and those of us who delight in intricacy might even find the resulting policies offered, intriguing.

If one of our presidential candidates were to seriously hammer away on these two issues, I could see ways to put together a real plan for change. He or she could pull in economic concerns by noting that jobs in both these service occupations are expanding. Health and education involve people to people interaction, and that interaction works best when the people are working closely together; so, most of these jobs can't be outsourced. Both need more workers—more teachers, nurses, doctors, medical personnel of all kinds. There's lots of loose talk about retraining those who will lose jobs to outsourcing, but not much about what the training ought to be. These areas could use new sources of personnel.

The emphasis on health and education would have the added benefit of de-emphasizing the foreign policy area, where we have gone so disastrously astray. It says nothing about policing the world, a white man's burden we need to drop as quickly as possible, preferably before we go broke. The country is tired of spending money on misdirected adventures like Iraq, when we have needs of our own. A president, who believes that the world ought to be involved in solving the world's problems, might make use of our growing awareness of the financial burden to encourage the building of alliances as opposed to the current administration's grandiose notions of empire. We should be more than ready to drop that nonsense and the military build-up, chest beating that goes with it. The money saved by adopting a sane and co-operative military policy should go primarily to health and education.

If you happen to be among those who consider global warming and other environmental concerns the issues we ought to emphasize, consider the environmental footprint of activities like health and education. At their core education and health are not high environmental impact areas of human activity. Of course there are schools and hospitals to be built, but those are ancillary activities. No one would argue that buildings are central to education and health in the same way that trucks, trains, and planes are central to transportation. Education could take place anywhere, in schools, in homes, in fire-houses etc. Healthcare is already spreading to small local facilities, and there is a growing emphasis on home care. Without trucks, trains or planes, there is no transportation. For both education and health care, the actual product consumed—learning or improved health—is about as impact free as any environmentalist could hope.

The next president will have to do something about medical insurance and he/she should do something about education. Perhaps the discussion could start by making clear that well educated, healthy people will produce just the sort of workers the US will need in order to compete in the new world economy. With healthy minds and healthy bodies, we can compete with anyone. If the next president is unable to lead with that line, he/she probably shouldn't be president. Add in some of the other benefits of putting our emphasis in these two areas, and I would think that the next president could develop a program that would make us all proud.

Praise for a Real American Victory

November 8, 2008

Barack Obama brought us a real American victory to celebrate by winning, with a significant if not over-whelming vote of approval, over a candidate who talked incessantly about a military victory in Iraq, where such a victory makes little sense. As I've written in previous blogs, victory over terrorists, (the McCain subtext to victory in Iraq), won't be military and won't happen in our lifetime. When poverty and inequality are more likely to increase than not, and when there are plenty of would-be dictators available world-wide to exploit the resulting bitterness, with weapons increasingly available and increasingly horrendous, we should not even talk about military victory over terrorism; we should talk about victorious ideas like the democratic election of 2008; we can police and contain but the concept of military victories is as hollow as Bush's aircraft carrier bravado.

Now we can talk about a significant victory, especially if we see this election as a victory over some of our own worst instincts or better as a step toward appreciating our own real strengths. The image that seems to stay with me (as idea after idea about the election swirls around in my brain and all too often tumbles in confusion all over the floor) came, surprisingly enough, from the mainstream media; Good Morning America, to be exact. They showed a clip previously taken at a Pennsylvania bowling alley, where Barack lost ground to Hillary by delivering a resounding gutter ball, in an awkward attempt to bind with the locals.

Every mainstream image we saw about the folks at the bowling alley, including this GMA clip, suggested that they were simply too unsophisticated to change their minds and vote for someone portrayed endlessly as an elitist, and there were even hints from the same sources that they would never vote for a black man. Well, the return visit by GMA, just before the election, showed them capable of an admirable practicality and, yes, sophistication. One man did admit, when questioned directly, that race would play a part in his vote, but I came away believing it wouldn't be a deciding part. He seemed to have figured out good reasons to leave any lingering racial reservations behind and to focus on issues more important to him. I came away convinced that he and his friends would vote for Barack, since voting for Hillary was no longer an option.

Apparently, they saw through 'you betcha' Sarah clearly too, even though she was supposed to appeal to them in particular. They changed their minds, something would-be intellectuals, like myself, find a lot more difficult than we like to admit. These Americans had to get past the guns and religion quote from Barack's fund raising speech in San Francisco.[30] I'd like to think I could rise above a similar comment directed at something I cherish, but I'm far from sure I could. These Americans did. They didn't even bite when McCain turned the progressive income tax ideal into socialism. They ignored McCain/Palin pandering, they overcame distrust, they weighed options; in other words, they thought things through and left gut reactions to Bush and McCain. I like to think they'll appreciate a president who thinks things through, too.

Of course the cynic in me can't help thinking GMA had staged yet another feel good moment, but today I'm too euphoric to listen to the downer within. So here's to American Democracy and

---

[30] "...they get bitter, they cling to guns or religion or antipathy to people who aren't like them or anti-immigrant sentiment or anti-trade sentiment as a way to explain their frustrations."

to the changes it allows us all to make in ourselves and then to express in a relatively orderly fashion.

The 2008 election results are a resounding answer to terrorism with far more power to isolate terrorists than misused military force. We are already hearing from an inspired world, ready and even anxious to forgive us after years of arrogant behavior by our current leaders. Goodbye Bush, goodbye Cheney, goodbye Wolfowitz, goodbye Perle, goodbye disdain for the rest of the world and for the intelligence of our own citizens and welcome to a government that will do its best to foster respect for the rest of the world and for the regular Joe voters in Pennsylvania and for the rest of us too.

President Obama's First Week

January 30, 2009

Barack Obama has been president for only one week, as I begin writing this entry. Yet, I find myself scarcely able to list, let alone analyze, what he has done so far. He's reasserted our country's long-standing dedication to the rule of law, rejecting the previous administration's positions on torture, habeas corpus, rendition, illegal wire-tapping, and politicizing of the justice department. He latched onto the world-wide symbol of the Bush administration's lawless[31] behavior by setting the timetable for closing Guantanamo. He's set a timetable for extricating us from Iraq, and he's focused our effort in Afghanistan on Al Qaeda, where we need to focus, instead of attempting to make a democracy out of a tribal society or a functioning economy out of an opium trade enclave. What a switch for the Secretary of Defense holdover, Mr. Gates.

He has reached out to the moderate Muslim world, not only in the inauguration speech, but also by making himself available to Al Arabiya for his first televised interview, and by appointing two seasoned diplomats—one for Afghanistan/Pakistan and the other for the Mid East. From the start he has indicated that the

---

[31] Technically, of course, the behavior becomes lawless only after it has been prosecuted, tried, and judged lawless. We ought to get on that. The conventional wisdom seems to be that prosecution right now might seem to Republicans like a Democratic witch hunt, just when we need their votes on other matters. I'm not sure that the law isn't more important than what Republicans might think; but, if we are not going to prosecute right now, let's at least set up a commission like the 9/11 commission to determine what the national policy on these issues ought to be. A New York Times op-ed piece suggested putting John McCain and any number of Republican military men on the commission to blunt the witch hunt attack. I could go with that, though I must admit that dunking might be just about right for the perpetrators of the Bush torture policies.

rest of the world matters and that our security is best preserved by grounding our approach to the world on our values. He's begun to express values based on his community organizing background, emphasizing that we have responsibilities to our fellow citizens and to the rest of the world, not just to ourselves.

He's laying the groundwork for rejecting the self fulfilling Reagan-era notion that government is the problem by attacking revolving door lobbying practices and by insisting that we are all responsible for our government. To help us assume that responsibility, he has declared government secrecy the exception, not the rule it became under Bush/Cheney; as responsible citizens, we will need accurate information about what our government is doing.

The whole attitude toward the rest of us has changed. We are not to be kept in the dark, guided only by our poppa Bush and super-poppa Cheney, those in the know. The lights are to be turned on government, and if we look and then do our part to see that government functions, we may even see regulatory agencies dedicated to regulating rather facilitating those they are supposed to oversee. He inspires us to keep alert and he shows us how to inspire others.

Already I'm seeing many of these initiatives described as symbolic, too often with an implied subtext that the merely symbolic is not as important as the substantive policies that must follow, or as important as what the Newark Star Ledger[32] listed as "the central missions of his presidency: overhauling health care, weaning the nation from foreign oil, and fixing the economy". The Ledger analysis went on to correct the implication that these early moves weren't important by listing political, tone setting, time buying, and world signaling effects, but still went back to the notion that policies to come are the real test.

I'd turn that notion on its head and say the real tests of presidential effectiveness are symbolic acts. What do we remember

---

[32] Newark Star Ledger, 1/25/09 by Peter Nicholas and Christi Parsons, Chicago Tribune.

about FDR? Is it the Fireside chats, the symbol of a new under-standing between the people and their government, or the alphabet soup of agencies that represented the policies? Will we remember Bush 2 for 'mission accomplished' and the Katrina flyby or for his AIDS policy, one of his few policy successes? Policies are hard work and they matter deeply, but presidencies often turn on leadership qualities that hinge on symbolic acts.

And, incidentally, there have been policy changes too. Obama has overturned some of the more abhorrent wilderness area rever-sals of the Bush administration.[33] He has broken the link between our offer of aid to poor countries and the rhythm method as the only acceptable contraception. It's a step toward allowing women some control over their lives where control is everywhere but in their own hands. Let's hope our new Secretary of State, a world leader for women's rights, builds on that first block. Just today, the economic assistance and recovery act or stimulus package passed the house, and he helped it along. As important, he has listened to Washington's Republican politicians and conservative pundits, coming away from the two meetings admired by both these potentially antagonistic groups for his ability to listen and to think. Listening to and thinking about opposing ideas has been in short supply within the governing circles over the last eight years.

I certainly hope that Obama doesn't act very often on what he hears from Republicans or conservatives these days. Upping tax breaks for businesses and the general working public at the expense of infrastructure spending as a form of stimulus seems to be their main contribution to the current debate, and we've heard that from them before, time and time again. Not much has trickled down from the businesses and far too many workers have been quite rightly scared into saving rather than inspired to stimulate the economy by spending. Conservative knee-jerk responses

---

[33] The Omnibus Public Land Management Act passed the Senate and now needs to pass in the House. It will be a big plus for wilderness area preservation and go well beyond what can be done by presidential authority alone.

need to be rejected, not encouraged. But you never know, they might come up with a new idea, or at least a practical suggestion or two, from time to time. At least we know this—New York Times op ed readers will be hearing nothing more from William Kristol (read knee-jerk conservative) and more from David Brooks (read thoughtful conservative)[34]; now that's an improvement. And, speaking of improvements, we now have a president and first lady promising to convert the Blue Room of the White House into an open area for jazz concerts, chamber music performances, and poetry readings. There's probably a conservative or two out there who could join with me in celebrating that kind of change.

---

[34] Brooks' piece today (1/30/09) attacks the stimulus bill as a hodge-podge, and he makes some good points. His assumption is that the stimulus will not be needed beyond this year, so projects that extend to 2010, 2011, and 2012 are not needed in this bill. I hope he's right about the length of this recession, but I'm not betting my financial planning on it. Besides, I think the longer-term projects are critical, and I'm not averse to sneaking them through in a stimulus bill. I can understand that as long-term Democratic objectives (real healthcare, energy sanity, and significant, national education spending) they might not appeal to David Brooks.

Our Congressional Representatives

February 20, 2010

Here's a scary thought, one that Newsweek chose to explore in several articles recently (2/15/2010). Our representatives actually do represent you and, even worse, me. My representative (Leonard Lance) is a Republican and I'm a firm Democrat. We have philosophical differences and policy differences that I've referred to often in this blog. So, though he is my representative in congress, he must represent a lot of you more than he does me, wouldn't you think?

He still clings to Milton Friedman, or some popular version of Friedman, I prefer Keynes or his reincarnation, Paul Krugman. I see money flowing up to a more and more concentrated elite as a significant societal danger; he seems to live in Republican land where the flow up, despite the fact that it defies gravity, is all hunky-dory, because it will trickle down someday. I don't think those in the bottom lands would go so far as to ask for a flood, but a trickle, even the wording sounds stingy.

Newsweek, though, had other notions of what "to represent" means. For me the strikingly simple point they made, in a number of ways and in separate articles, is that our representatives represent the fundamental contradiction we all share to some degree when we think about what we expect from our government. We expect the same or even increased services and we expect lower taxes. We expect solutions to very large problems, but we are not willing to pay up for whatever solutions to those problems our representatives may discuss. We blithely drive the interstate, across bridges that are crumbling, and then begrudge or label as pork any funds to repair them, prior to a disaster. We love solar and wind power, and we grumble at anything like adequate funding, especially if our representative suggests something like a windmill farm or a massive solar array in our backyard.

In fact, during the Bush years, our representatives have perfectly reflected our astounding illogic by not only promising too much for too little but by delivering benefits without a thought of paying. They've handed us Medicare drug benefits and thrown in two wars, and then actually reduced taxes. And, we have not spontaneously generated a grass roots movement to increase taxes while we continue to gobble up the services and tolerate the wars. In fact we've created just the opposite, endless tax cut movements, parties and websites.

Recently I thought to amuse a libertarian friend by suggesting that he join me in the increase taxes movement. Too bad he has the only logical answer to oppose such a movement; "forget more government services, I don't need them," I think he would say. I assume he drives back roads in a jeep and fords streams; I didn't ask. I only wish I had an equally solid answer, that I would be willing to walk the walk, as well as talk the talk, when it comes to the other logical response, my increase taxes movement.

Perhaps I need to think about increased taxes more personally. It might mean giving up my home mortgage tax break. As a child of the IRA era, without a pension, if I were to be at all honest, I'd have to consider increased taxes on interest, dividends, and capital gains. Now that would hurt. I'm all for a progressive income tax, so those making way more than they could possibly need can help by paying a greater proportion of their income to help cover our common expenses, but that wouldn't hurt me. A consumption tax or value added tax? Bring it on, I say, knowing full well that I'm well past my heavy consuming years. That 'bring it on' would ring as hollow as it did when George W. Bush said it about the Iraq war. I'll have to wait for the increase taxes ground swell to sweep along some of you out there who would be hit hard by high income, consumption, or value added taxes, before we can make those alternatives credible. Hello there, ready to join the movement? Warren Buffett and George Soros, I believe, may have already signed on.

Unfortunately our representatives share several other limitations with us. In fact, one—short term thinking—is built into our representatives' two year election cycle. They have that extra incentive, beyond representing us all too accurately, to think short term. My wife often points out that longer term thinking is a lot harder for someone barely scraping by, someone with children in need of constant and immediate attention, someone who doesn't sit around all day reading newspapers and magazines, researching obscure historical movements, or writing blogs, like me. When she really gets going on the subject she's apt to point out that I have no knowledge of what it's like to be struggling without much hope that the struggle will ever end.

She's right, of course. I'm constantly re-awakened, when I read about those who actually are stuck in perpetual struggles. Reading recently in the AARP magazine, about a man wiped out by medical problems, provided one of those wake up jolts. I wasn't surprised by the fact that medical problems destroyed his life, that's too common in our country to surprise anyone. What shocked me is that his lifetime savings were $40,000.00. He was headed for a life of struggles without medical problems; no retirement for him. Do I have any right to expect him to consider fine points of long term thinking like whether our climate issues should be called global warming, climate change, or climate 'weirding', as Thomas Friedman suggested in The Times recently?

Maybe I have no right to expect those mired in daily struggles to think longer term, but that exemption does not apply to my representative. Last I heard both his retirement benefits and his medical insurance were top of the line. In fact I think I have a right to expect him to think long term and to talk to us sensibly about our long term problems. Despite the two year cycle, getting re-elected is not his only responsibility to his constituents. We might even go so far as to expect him to take the lead in thinking long term. Instead he seems content to mirror our vaguest fears about the budget deficit without even hinting at a viable plan of action beyond the usual inadequate Republican talking points.

I don't even know where he stands on other long term issues like climate change, and I follow him more closely than most. He did join in the request to investigate the so called climate gate emails, using that inflammatory designation specifically, and he did support a modest house bill to establish renewable energy credits for electric utilities. However, I cannot find one reference to his specific beliefs about climate change science, positive or negative. Leadership requires more specificity than that. It requires looking at all sides of an argument, providing explanations and suggestions, choosing a side, and then advocating action or not.

I will say that my representative is not so insensitive to his district as to join in the general attack on those who do the detailed, ground work research on which sensible arguments are based. He doesn't attack intellectuals as opposed to regular guys and gals, an attack favored by tea party activists, Sarah Palin, and far too many commentators. He is not a one liner looking for easy targets in order to stir up hate. None-the-less, his reference to climate-gate does seem disturbing. It echoes the anti-intellectual line without being as obviously tacky as Palin. It suggests, as his announcement on the subject made a bit too clear, that there may be something to the notion that scientists lack integrity, that they can be bought, and that therefore their science is suspect. Once that notion takes hold with the public, and especially if the knee jerk distrust spreads to other intellectuals like economists, say, then there will be no one to turn to for the kind of reliable information needed to think and act long term.

Perhaps, therefore, we should consider just what an intellectual, and by extension, what a scientist is, before Sarah's definition—a college educated smart aleck who looks down with disdain on the regular folk—fills the definition vacuum. I've been updating my own definition. I now think that an intellectual is someone who keeps digging into a subject, any subject, so deeply that the Internet, despite its immense collection of information, is no longer able to provide the data needed. Research, for an intellectual, hits walls, and the only answers become ones the intellectual provides, often through acts of creativity, or through digging where others lacked the persistence to dig. Intellectuals are long term investigators into problems[35]; they're curious, persistent, exacting, and, if true to their calling, open to admitting mistakes, and then open to trying again. They are not the easiest humans to corrupt; their passion for exactitude helps to protect them.

Can scientists and other intellectuals be corrupted? Of course they can. More insidiously they can suffer, at times, from group-think. Are they sometimes dumber than other folk? Often and in many, many ways.[36] But when anyone implies, as I think the climategate talk does, that intellectuals including scientists can be corrupted on a wide scale, those who make such statements had better be as diligent as most intellectuals are in seeking out the facts. It's not as if we have any other reliable basis for making decisions on issues like the economy, climate change, pollution, invasive species or any number of subjects none of us have sufficient time to investigate, even if we are retired and waste time writing

---

[35] Click and Clack, the tappet brothers, (NPR) answered a call from a thermo-nuclear physicist from Princeton. They had great fun discussing the fact that given his subject matter, he would always remain a failure. Nothing practical is expected from this research in the lifetimes of anyone older than 10. The whole effort may fail. Now that's long-term thinking.

[36] The same caller as above owned a 1991 Ford Escort and asked whether he should change the timing belt as recommended or not. Click and Clack suggested that he could just let it go as he had been doing, but if the car suddenly stopped on the Jersey Turnpike, they would not be there to pick him up off the pavement once two or three semis ran over him without really noticing. Dumb. Dumb to take chances with your life for the cost of a timing built. Not too smart to be driving a 1991 Escort, still, though I hope, myself, to match his persistence by holding on to my '98 Dodge.

blogs. In the end, we need to put our faith in some institutions, and for me that's internationally respected scientific institutions, research universities, and other organizations with a history of impartiality to protect.

Interview with Representative Leonard Lance

April 4, 2010

I know you have all been patiently awaiting an update on my 'increase taxes' movement first mentioned in my 2/20/2010 blog entry. The movement has definitely suffered setbacks here in central NJ. In fact the setbacks are bad enough that I might be tempted to remove my pro-tax bumper sticker. A recent survey on the subject conducted by my Republican congressman, Leonard Lance, came up with the following results:

The results of the poll are in with nearly 2,400 respondents:
1,661 respondents said they pay too much in taxes;
491 respondents said they pay just enough in taxes;
80 respondents said they pay too little in taxes; and
109 were undecided.

Note that only 79 respondents, besides me, out of 2,400 felt they did not pay enough; the movement has a long way to go. Here's what my representative had to say about his own positions:

"I believe New Jerseyans pay too much in taxes. New Jersey also has the highest state and local tax burden, the second highest business tax burden and the state collects more property taxes per capita than any other jurisdiction.

For my part, I support renewing the soon-to-expire 2001 and 2003 Bush tax cuts, and have been a vocal opponent to the president's plan to raise taxes on New Jerseyans making $250,000 or more.

I voted in favor of fully eliminating the "death tax" and am a cosponsor of legislation to repeal the onerous Alternative Minimum Tax (AMT). New Jersey's Seventh District is in the top 10 of congressional districts whose constituents are adversely affected by the AMT."

How Jerseyeans do suffer, especially those who own homes (and pay those local real estate taxes), make over $250,000 a year (and cringe at the thought of a minuscule income tax increase), look forward to multi-million dollar inheritances (and might have to end up paying estate taxes), and finagle enough deductions to get hit by the AMT.[37] The burden on these folks is really insufferable, and our representative is actively addressing this seriously unfair attack on those who support the New Jersey yachting industry.[38]

Yes, I do understand that there are home owners in trouble and that the AMT needs adjustments so that it doesn't hit those who earn what have now become middling incomes, but I'm still betting that most of the people in these categories aren't the neediest among us. Basically, I'm in a charitable frame of mind today, so I'd like to believe that a good number of those other 79 who said they didn't pay enough taxes and some of the 491 who thought their taxes were ok might just be among the yachting set and really aren't looking for a tax break from their representative.

I find my representative's statement on taxes even more difficult to comprehend after talking to him personally in a one-on-one exchange a couple of weeks ago. I had come into the interview with figures on the Bush tax cuts gathered mainly from

[37] The AMT is a baffling alternate tax system with its own deduction rules. I don't pretend to understand the details. Thanks to Turbo Tax I've never felt the need to understand them.

[38] Full disclosure might require me to mention that I own a boat and often keep it at a marina. Yacht would be a stretch; it's more a tent camper not the stateroom sort of craft. I'm thinking, here, of the NYC Yacht Club crowd made famous by the Tom Paxton song about the America's cup. "They lost the cup, you say, did they lose the saucer too?"

Paul Krugman's <u>The Great Unraveling</u>. Here's that section from my talking point notes:

A. Reagan/ George W. Bush—Cut taxes, starve the beast—? Which taxes?
1. Payroll tax = 15.3%, income to $70,000. Payroll tax includes Social Security, Medicare, and disability. I'm not clear whether the percentage figure includes both what the employee pays and what the employer pays. That 15.3% would seem to imply that Krugman included both. Payroll tax is the largest tax for 4 out of 5 workers, according to Krugman (2002 figures)—No Bush tax cut.
2. Income tax = less than 10% for most families, up to 30% for about 1 million people at top rate. Large Bush tax cut, for top earners. About 1% of small businesses benefit from this tax cut.
3. Estate tax. Hits 2% of estates. Mostly paid by a few 1000 multi-millionaires. Bush tax cut eliminates the estate tax until 2010.

My point, and Krugman's, is that the Bush tax cuts had little to do with lowering taxes for most citizens. For most workers the larger tax is the payroll tax for disability, Social Security and Medicare. No Bush cut for that tax. Income tax? Here's where the Bush tax cut really excelled, but not for most tax payers. It was a high end tax cut and the idea was that it would aid small business, increase GDP, trickle down to workers, and cure our economic ills through growth. That didn't happen, perhaps in part because only 1% of small businesses actually benefited. Finally the Bush tax cuts took care of multi-millionaires by eliminating the estate tax, ensuring that they could pass along their wealth to the next generation.

Go back and reread Representative Leonard Lance's statements on his tax program and you will see how closely it resembles the Bush tax plan. No surprise there, it's the Republican tax plan, and it has been for a long time. What surprised me is that during our conversation he completely agreed that the disparity between the yachting crowd (I didn't use that term in the interview) and a large majority of US citizens has seldom been so great. He mentioned the year or so before the great depression as perhaps the last time the difference equaled today's. Somehow this extreme concentration of wealth at the top didn't seem to disturb him as much as it does me. I guess I have visions of regimes that end up toppling when massive numbers of those without means get so angry they actually revolt. Tea Parties, after-all, have a revolutionary history. I'd prefer some balance with a strong middle class to stabilize society. It's hard to see how the Bush tax plan or the Leonard Lance tax plan would redress the balance; in fact, just the opposite.

In fairness I need to add that Representative Lance did state that he thought both Republicans and Democrats had been fiscally irresponsible. Neither party had really addressed the difference between what we are willing to spend and what we are willing to pay for. The only positive actions on this front he mentioned were the Clinton fiscal policies; though he wanted to be sure I understood that he thought Newt Gingrich deserved a portion of the credit. His position on the estate tax (inheritance, death tax) was more moderate when he discussed it with me, too. He did not seem to insist on elimination; instead he suggested that an increase in the size of the estates to be subjected to the tax might provide some middle ground on the issue. I'm thinking he might agree to an adjustment to the AMT, also, though we didn't discuss specifics.

Even if my representative's more nuanced views were more prominent in his public pronouncements, I would still find it hard to understand how he and Republicans in general manage to sell their lopsided tax breaks for the 'elite' to the majority of Americans. I've gotten a clue, though, recently. Just the other day a Pew survey came out with the not too surprising fact (given media coverage of the Tea Party) that 80% of Americans do not trust their federal government 'to do the right thing'. That's the lowest trust level ever reached since the question was first asked during the Eisenhower administration. One is forced to see a certain degree of logic in asking whether the federal government should get any money if they aren't going to do the right thing with it. If one feels that way about the government, then who pays them is not as critical an issue.

One would hope that someone would think to ask what the right thing might be. In fact that was the next question I put to Representative Lance in our interview. I had prepared somewhat copiously in my notes outlining those items that I felt would not offend the most conservative of economists—the Adam Smith, Milton Friedman crowd. We expect our government to provide protection from threats from external powers, whether the threats are military or economic. We expect a certain amount of protection from those among our own citizens who would if unchecked take unfair advantage of law abiding citizens or businesses. We even expect government to step-in when projects crucial to our security or economic viability are of such size and duration as to exceed the free market's ability to risk financing them. Think the interstate highway system. So far that's straight out of Adam Smith and Milton Friedman. Friedman even went so far as to suggest that those crushed by the free enterprise system might deserve some government relief.

Unfortunately, the interview was only ½ hour and I got stuck on one of my own ideas about the role of government, leaving out a host of more liberal ideas. I started the discussion by relating my favorite Milton Friedman free market story. Friedman describes in considerable detail how the free market deals with the manufacture of a pencil. He describes the complexity of the market starting with raw materials like the cedar for the wooden part of the pencil. There's machinery for harvesting trees, shipping, oil for the ships, gas for the saws, manufacturing, distribution, marketing, sales—best to leave such complexity be, government would just mess up such an intricate set of relationships. Besides the free market is self regulating. Suppose the system runs into a supply side problem, cedar trees begin to become scarce and therefore more expensive. The system handles that for a while by adjusting the price until people begin to wonder if a wood and lead pencil is really worth the money. Is it still a value? No, well then, some entrepreneur comes along and invents, manufactures, and markets a better value, the mechanical pencil, say.

This traditional economic theory presents us with a really elegant sounding system until you ask, as I did, after telling a shortened version to Representative Lance—what about those cedar trees? The theory relies on a definition of value that includes only what someone is willing to pay for the object itself. Nowhere is there any value assigned to the consequences of production. If every cedar tree were consumed, if mudslides running down denuded hillsides eliminated whole towns, if workers in the forests were slaves[39], no matter, this value theory is untouched. We now know, or should know, that everything we produce has consequences beyond what this traditional theory values, even the mechanical pencil.

When I asked Representative Lance whether he thought a 21st century definition of value might emerge out of an updated consideration of the consequences of production, he seemed to understand the point. When I asked who might be responsible for adding such considerations to the value of objects produced, he drew the only blank of the whole interview. I could hardly blame him; he may not hear this question every day. He picked right up though when I mentioned a specific example, cap and trade to compensate for the consequences of burning fossil fuels. I think he was happy to mention that he was one of only 8 Republicans

---

[39] I haven't followed up on earlier concerns about the state of foreign workers enticed to the Mariana Islands by the hope of working under the American flag and under its recognized labor laws. These are the workers kept caged up and cheated out of their wages by unscrupulous employers. Our US labor laws do not extend to US territories, or they didn't when Tom Delay praised these employers as excellent examples of free market entrepreneurs.

to vote for the House version of cap and trade. Note, he doesn't mention this vote too often, here, in Republican central Jersey.

Maybe once my representative sees the connection between cap and trade as compensation for the consequences of burning fossil fuel and the wider issue of including compensation for other consequences in what we define as the value of an object, he'll move on and become one of my tax champions. I've decided to help him along toward this point of view by extending my campaign to include the Value Added Tax (VAT) movement, now largely a think tank concept in the US, though it's been implemented substantially in Europe. Representative Lance opposes it currently. After-all, any tax is a hard sell here, and the VAT may suffer even more than other taxes in part because of its wonky name.

The name is based on the method of collecting the tax, not exactly an inspiring motive for adopting it. The way it is collected is interesting, though. At each step in the production process, a tax is assessed, and then at the next step the amount of the tax paid in the previous step can be deducted from the tax due at the current step. Each step in the production process has an interest in seeing to it that the previous step has paid its tax and recorded that payment accurately. Wow, it's self-regulating; now why wouldn't a Republican like that? Those who calculate such things believe that collecting this tax would be far less expensive and onerous than the income tax.

Cheers from Republicans and the rest of us for VAT, or did eyes glaze over in boredom? I have serious doubts that I understand it myself or care deeply about the details. What I would understand and, more important, care about is what the VAT could stand for. We'll re-brand it right here and now as the Value Adjusted Tax (VAT). Each step in the production process contributes something to compensate for the currently undervalued costs to society in general of producing an object. Funds collected could be targeted to relieving the effects of production—to environmental preservation, disaster relief, an end to slavery or other forms of employment exploitation—all those messy, little side effects Milton Friedman neglected to include in his original and oh so tidy definition of value. Oh, yes, nod to my Representative; perhaps we might pay off some of our debt before we spend it all.

Republicans cringe at any thought of a tax increase, as do most Americans, so I have an idea that might make an increase more palatable. Albert A. Foer, in a Times op-ed (4/21/10), points out that credit card companies in the US charge about 2% to merchants for our use of credit cards and debit cards. Does American Express charge even more? His solution to this somewhat extravagant financial company cut of the pie is two-fold. Since debit cards are really just plastic checks against an existing account, and since banks are not allowed to charge each time we cash a paper check, there is no reason to allow this plastic check charge. For credit cards, since there is a service provided and risk taken, some amount is due to Visa and Master Charge etc… However, he argues that 2% is about 1.5% too much. He further points out that some countries already regulate this amount; Australia set the rate at 0.5%. Their regulation has been in effect for 5 years, and it works.

So what does this have to do with the Value Adjusted Tax (VAT)? Why not implement both at the same time? Decreasing the debit/credit card charge would save merchants money offsetting to a considerable degree the extra they would need to charge to cover VAT expenses. Keep in mind that the tax is surely going to pass on to the consumer; in Australia the savings from the credit card expense reduction did too. Though I'm not enough of an economist to figure out whether they would simply cancel each other out, still, a tax that hurts the consumer a lot less than anticipated can't be all bad. Also I'm guessing that Republicans, burned by their defense of extravagant bank profits, now that the Goldman Sachs scandal has broken, might think twice at the thought of running to the rescue of the extravagant profits Visa and Master Card take directly out of our pockets.

It's One Country

July 1, 2011

For some reason, unknown to me, I've been thinking about the Mississippi River and all its many tributaries—the Ohio, the Missouri, the Arkansas, the Illinois, the Minnesota, the Rock, the St. Croix, the Kaskaskia, the White, and the Red—along with their tributaries too numerous even for me to list. Maybe it was the floods, or maybe I'm just getting too old and spend too much time reminiscing; I did once take a paddle wheeler up the river from St. Louis to St. Paul. It's a natural wonder of awe inspiring proportions, this center of the nation scooped out by the Laurentide glacial ice sheet. The whole system covers 31 states, right in the middle of our country. It ought to serve us as our national emblem of connectedness.

Throughout our history we have been adding to these natural connectors, first by supplementing the rivers with canals, then by adding railroads, and then by creating a national highway system (under Eisenhower, the last Republican president who seemed to embody our common sense of purpose). Given such a clear history of ever increasing physical connections, you would think the whole country, even the East and West coasts, would be forced to think of itself as one nation.

And yet, with the Mississippi, such an apt emblem of these connections, running through their souls and affecting their very existence, it seems that the central section of our country contains a disproportionate number of people who do not cherish our connectedness with the ardor their location cries out for them to recognize. Instead they tend toward an odd, to me anyway, reliance on the most arbitrary of divisions; they just seem to love loyalty to state lines as opposed to the real contours of their environment.

Wisconsin and Iowa, I still haven't figured out how the Wisconsin territory became two states, or was it more, I can't remember; probably had something to do with political balances of the time. I'd be ok with state loyalties if they didn't seem to come coupled with state centered attitudes. One might expect 'we're different, leave us alone' from real outliers like Alaskans, and you'd be right; but from the Midwest, such an outlandish loyalty to arbitrary lines and the associated assumption of separateness does not make sense to me.

Oh, yes, I know, we're a federation, an association of states under the constitution, sort of like our original confederation. But, the confederation failed, and the next time around the founding fathers made sure that the central government had the wherewithal to overcome state bound idiosyncrasies and peculiar institutions, when necessary. When rebels tried to insist that they had the right to resist federal power, presidents who knew how to lead, from Washington to Lincoln to Kennedy and Johnson, crushed rebellion, even when the rebels had state backing. And yet certain state politicians still argue, as Calhoun did before the Civil War, that states have the right to nullify federal laws within their boundaries. Where have they been living? Did they notice who won the Civil War? What kind of antiquated mindset clutters the musty attic of their minds?

Actually, levels of government, from town to county to state to federal, work really well when responsibilities are clearly defined and disputes are settled within a sensible legal system that we all recognize and respect. In fact multiple layers encourage a variety of approaches, provide proving grounds for ideas, like the Massachusetts, public/private Healthcare plan or Vermont's proposed single payer plan.

We do differ across such a varied country, and various levels of government allow us to approach problems differently. Our differences do not have to be counter-productive. They can lead to acceptance on the federal level of such long overdue attempts at universal coverage as the Affordable Health Care Act, or, perhaps in a few more decades on to something like what may become Vermont's single payer plan.

Unfortunately, though, for some citizens, the federal system tends to encourage a habit of thinking that all problems or at least too many problems are better left to localized solutions. It's so much easier to associate with smaller governmental entities— state, county, local—than with far away Washington. However, most of our real problems these days simply do not fit neatly into such a mindset. Fertilizer spread irresponsibly on a field in Iowa without proper buffering seeps into a local stream, works its way down a tributary of a tributary into the Mississippi, and flows on down to the gulf where the algae just love it, but people who fish the gulf do not. Local sewage systems poorly maintained wreck havoc on neighbors downstream. From global warming to acid rain to nitrogen pollution to sewage to plastic bags, the environment is not simply a local matter.

Those who attack Washington, whenever the EPA finally gets around to addressing environmental issues, tend to be the same people who deny environmental problems. Environmental problems are so clearly national and even global that denying the existence of the problems is their only logical option consistent with their misdirected detestation of what they see as Washington's interference in their states, their local communities and their personal lives. At the extreme end of the spectrum, you end up with pandering drivel like Michele Bachmann's recent promise during the first Republican campaign debate to do away with the EPA altogether. Full retreat from reality is comforting, and she hawks her bromides well.

Or, maybe I'm wrong about what such people think. Maybe they honestly believe that solutions to national or global problems must percolate up from the grass roots before those solutions become viable. We're a democracy, after-all, and democracies work by gaining wide base support for action before any action is taken. It's a slow and frustrating system, but it's better than any of the alternatives. I've argued so myself. Sometimes, though, we can't wait forever. Since Rachel Carson's 'The Silent Spring', written in the 50's, we've known we have environmental problems. That knowledge is so common that it has seeped into our educational system; ask any kid and you will hear about what mommy and daddy should be doing to save the environment.

And yet, mommy and daddy seldom take the simplest everyday environmentally responsible action they could on their own, without any government interference from any level. Just walk into any grocery store and count how many customers bring cloth bags. It's one of my own little tics to note this. In the liberal Princeton NJ area, where I often shop, on a good day, you'd be lucky to count 1 in 15. Move a little north to Hillsborough, Republican territory, and 1 in 30 would be a remarkable day. Take a jaunt down to the Shenandoah's, where I am enjoying a week of camping in this jewel of a federal park; and, based on what is obviously a snap judgment, I'm guessing you will not see one cloth bag.

Paper bags don't exist down here, except at Chipotle's, a known green chain. Grocery stores don't even carry paper bags. If they did, I'm fairly confident that folks down here would do what too many in New Jersey do, double bag with a paper bag inside a plastic. I have only seen one person, in many years of observing, who carries easily available mesh bags for packaging produce like lettuce or oranges before they get to the plastic infested, checkout counter.

I'm not at all apologetic about this, you anti-Washington folk, it's time to wake up and pass the San Francisco law outlawing plastic bags altogether, nationally. You had your chance to do it your way, and you failed. Give me federal government intrusion over plastic bag havoc, now. No more Pacific Ocean currents of plastic. No more, oh we'll recycle those plastic bags. Do you do it? Not often enough. If you did, would it eliminate the plastic catastrophe that fills our landfills, litters our landscape, and pollutes our oceans? No. Plastic lasts forever, whether it's converted to more plastic bags, plastic furniture, or whatever, it ends up as plastic waste, and it seriously denigrates the environment for ages into the future.

What I'd like to say is that plastic has no place in the 21st Century. Fortunately, saner members of my family point out how critical plastic has become. Think of medical delivery devices, lots of plastic and no real alternatives. So, I'm reduced to insisting that where there are alternatives, we should use them. Where there are no current alternatives, we should spend real effort inventing them. I'm thinking bamboo is an underused material that could replace plastic chairs, for instance. I wonder what else we might do with it.

Enough on the environment, you say. But I say the environment is the primary 21st century disaster, unfolding right now, as we try desperately to ignore it. The Pentagon recognizes this. As the environment deteriorates, more countries slide into desperation, more people starve, more rebel, more seek radical alternatives, and the world becomes less secure. It's a circle of related issues that have the potential to rapidly spin out of control. Already scientists talk more about containment than avoidance.

We have entered what many scientists are labeling as a new geological age, the Anthropocene age.[40] Unlike former geological ages, this one did not take eons to evolve. It's a man made geological age that took only hundreds of years to burst upon us. We have only a proportionate time to evolve in response. If we have not replaced fossil fuels by 2050, I think we will have failed our children and our grand- children in a way that dwarfs any budget deficit we may leave them. We need a nationally directed effort, on the order of the Manhattan Project, to address energy needs. We can do this. It's possible. But, we cannot do it thinking locally; we need to think nationally, despite what head-in-the-sand localistas may think. In fact, horror of horrors for those who cling to small

[40] See 'The Economist', May 28th-June 3rd, for an excellent summary.

government, we need to develop global approaches to these problems and global governmental bodies to implement those approaches. We need bigger government entities, not smaller.

Think of it this way. At first the river system, the canals, and other transportation systems connected us as a nation along with nationally based communication systems—the telegraph, the telephone, the radio, television.[41] Now, we have the internet with worldwide information and social networks to connect us. Government structures have always limped somewhat slowly behind other forms of inter-connectedness, but eventually government catches up. Greater international cohesion is coming, folks, and you might as well recognize the potential for the good global governing bodies and international law will bring, and temper your distaste accordingly.

---

[41] An excellent history of the 19th Century traces the influence of transportation and communication as the country developed. See What Has God Wrought—the Transformation of America, 1815-1848 by Daniel Walker Howe. The title repeats the first words communicated over the telegraph in 1848.

CHAPTER 4
Our Place in the New World Order

Introduction

November, 2011

Recently, human being number 7 billion was born. I'd like to think we're ready. I'd like to think we are seriously preparing for the all too soon to arrive 8th billion. So many basic needs are multiplying way faster than we seem able to evolve to provide for them that I'd say we are not ready for seven billion and not preparing nearly seriously enough for eight.

What are we doing? Well, we've increased food production significantly, but we'd be hard put to argue that, remarkable as the increase has been, we are keeping up with current need let alone future need. Trying to keep up has required massive use of chemical fertilizers and increased use of marginal land or forest land, serious strains on our environment. Lots of that newly converted farm land is now going to production of bio-fuels instead of food. Lots of it feeds animals for meat production rather than grains to eat directly, a wasteful use we may come to regret.

Water supplies, energy supplies, whatever we need, or think we need, will feel the strain too. Areas in Africa suffer severely now from water supply problems and projections indicate there is worse to come. Our own western US of A has had and still has serious water supply issues. Global warming will aggravate water problems, particularly in the areas where the problems are most severe already. Need for energy from fuels will increase on the demand side and on the supply side we simply can't assume that new energy sources will keep up.

Think of the one issue that most directly leads to the population explosion—women who have no control over their lives let alone their reproductive lives. They produce so many more children in societies where they lack power than where they are empowered. And, what did we do about that? For eight years of the Bush administration we suggested the rhythm method, as if women in the third world had choices about their sexual lives. I see that idiocy as an indication of just how blind we can be when we isolate ourselves from the realities out there in the rest of the world.

Try as we might to isolate ourselves from the rest of mankind's approach to these issues, we simply cannot continue to ignore the obvious fact that what happens elsewhere affects us more directly than ever before.

So What's a Democrat to Do?

February 14, 2008

This Democrat made his choice on super-Tuesday in New Jersey; but decided, hardly. I'm a bit serious about my politics, as my blog entries surely indicate; so I struggle with the current Obama vs. Clinton decision, even after choosing on primary day. How do I decide whether I made the right choice or the wrong choice? To whom do I send my paltry campaign contribution? I refuse to decide on electability, race or gender; that much I know. I refuse to be swayed by the fact that the Republican candidate would love to take advantage of Hillary pillorying; I can't let the other party make my decision. Though I'm an issue geek, I believe in inspiration; I do remember the Kennedys, Jack and Robert.

I can't help it, I've got to start, at least, with issues; and I think any decision will need to turn on who can move forward with what I consider the major issues of our times. Make no mistake, this is important to me, because I believe my country is at one of those few moments in history when a major turn in the way we conceive of ourselves must occur. These moments don't come all that often—the civil war, the depression, WWII, the late 50's/60's environmental movement, the sixties civil rights movement (African Americans and women)—yes, I'm of the sixties and proud of it. There are a number of necessary turning points in our attitude to consider. Al Gore would choose either our attitude toward consumption and global warming or our attitude toward reason and the constitution. It's hard to argue with his emphasis on needed, major change in these areas, after 7 years of an administration without a clue about either.

As much as I admire Al Gore's definition of the changes required, I think I have another issue that will help me decide and that will be, if possible, even harder to confront for most of us. I formed this issue into concrete terms last week, though I had some abstract sense of it long ago. Consuelo Mack of "Wealth Track" helped crystallize it for me with some very stark figures. Currently the percentage of worldwide total GDP of developed countries vs. the others is 57% developed vs. 43% others. Oh, we are doing so well, bully. By 2050, the projections indicate that the percentages will be 23% for developed countries vs. 77% for currently undeveloped countries, the others. Oh shxx, we ain't top dog no more.

Nothing I've seen so far indicates so clearly, as these figures, that we need to start the process of adjusting to a different world order. So far we have been presented with two basic reactions. Bush, McCain and too many Republicans emphasize our military strength; over-powering brute force would seem to be the path they are currently on. Other empires have followed that path. Caesar's crossing of the Rubicon with soldiers by his side comes to mind as the essential moment when Rome went from a Republic to a military dictatorship. That's not a great path to my way of thinking. The alternative is what Republicans tend to portray as the mushy way; some difficult to define, singularly un-photogenic combination of alliance building, diplomacy, and quite a bit of that good old hard work Hillary tends to emphasize.

Of course the best path involves some carefully balanced recognition that two roads need not diverge in a murky wood. We'll need a military; we'll need better diplomats and more of them. But if we are headed toward becoming one of many influential countries rather than top dog, as seems to me inevitable, do we really need the lopsided military component we now maintain? If we develop allies, couldn't they pick up their portion of our mutual defense needs before we go further broke than we already are picking up their share too? Maybe we could get Saudi Arabia to finance Reagan's Star War fantasies; that would save us a bundle.

I remember the military strategy arguments that boiled down to whether we needed to prepare for two major conflicts at once or whether preparing for one would be sufficient. I'd always argued that preparing for two was the best way to end up fighting two. Bush, to our immense detriment, proved me right on that one.

What size military will we need? We need one sized to fit into an integrated global force ready to deal with events worldwide. Maybe if we have one sized in anticipation of allied contributions, we'd actually get those contributions, and we'd wait until we really had allies ready to do the job with us before rushing into quagmires. Think about selling that notion to a good portion of the US public, and just how far away we are from even talking about these issues becomes clear.

Talk about a third rail of politics, reducing the military is way worse as a matter for political discussion than Social Security. None of the candidates would touch it. So, how do we get to the point of facing up to our reduced position in the world as it becomes more and more clear? Hillary stumbled into an answer when she pointed out that it took a good politician to enact civil rights legislation. It did; Johnson lost the Democratic South doing it, and he and maybe he alone had the political talent to get it done, knowing it was political suicide. What Hillary forgot to emphasize was the other, far more important part of what makes change possible—the more difficult and drawn out job of changing the country's mind. King and so many others did that, as Barack reminded us and Hillary should have.

If I'm right in seeing our place in a world of multiple power centers, many with alien cultures, as the most important issue we need to face, then, at least one question is— exactly where are we in that discussion? And the answer is—not very far along. The Martin Luther King, Jr. we need to help us see this issue hasn't even arrived on the scene. Sometimes a president can help us see the issue clearly and execute an appropriate policy based on the vision. FDR did it twice, he saw what needed to be done to deal with the great depression and did it, then he saw that we needed to shed our isolation from the rest of the world and led us, step by step, to oppose fascism in WWII. The prophet, the fox, and the lion—such talents don't come along too often. I'm not expecting them to appear this year.

Given what I see as the most important issue and given where we are in discussing it, I'll wind on back to the original question, for whom should I have voted? We are clearly in the vision phase in terms of the 'our place in the world' discussion. The obvious answer is that I should vote for Barack Obama, the popularly anointed candidate of vision. But I'd come to that conclusion only if I thought he could take us the whole way from helping us see and understand the future, to convincing others to take a few steps, and finally on to implementing a coherent policy. Would that I could believe that he's the FDR of our times and could do it all, but I can't yet.

I think Barack Obama would serve us better out there for a number of years as an eloquent Al Gore speaking for change, figuring out the right changes, fleshing out some policy options, laying the groundwork for the politician who will need to implement. Right now I think that bringing the country the news of what's to come is even more important than being president, and I think he is the man to do it. Let Hillary do what she does best by implementing policies she and others have already worked out; policies that are ready or nearly ready for implementation like universal health care and reinstituting a progressive income tax. With a treasury depleted by the Bush and Chaney war policies and tax cuts for the wealthy, it will be hard enough to get these two tasks done in the next four years.

So, you ask, for whom did I vote on super-Tuesday? Well, so far Bush and Cheney haven't decided that our security depends on their access to that information; it remains one of the few areas of privacy they've left us, so I think I'll keep it that way. Incidentally, Hillary might want to work on basic respect for the law and constitution too, as Al Gore suggests; we might be ready for a few baby steps along that path, after 7 years of disrespect.

Message to Barack Obama

February 18, 2008

Here's what I sent to the Barack Obama My Space blog. It's slightly different from the one I sent Hillary because my reading of what they had to say is slightly different.

"I've read much of what is on the Obama website about our relations with the rest of the world, and I agree with what I believe to be the general, multilateral direction taken. However, I do not believe we need an increased military, if we believe in a multilateral approach. If we really do intend to be much more cautious in the use of unilateral military options, can't we resize our military with that plan in mind?

I remember the old arguments about whether we should be prepared for two major conflicts or one, and I had argued that planning for two makes fighting two more likely; and, of course, President Bush ended up doing so. I'd also argue that we could hedge against precipitous use of unilateral force if we sized our military for multilateral operations.

The cost of maintaining a military that is sized for a member of the world community rather than for an empire builder brings up the 2nd comment. "Wealth Track" had some interesting figures a couple of weeks ago based on the percentage of current world-wide GDP vs. 2050 projections for currently developed countries and other countries. The breakdown went like this:

	Current % GDP	2050 Projection
Current Developed Countries	57%	23%
Others	43%	77%

If nothing else convinces us that we need the rest of the world to solve problems requiring military action, eventually the money will. I'd prefer to see a candidate out there with the vision and the courage to advocate a military sized to provide what we need, preferably before we go broke maintaining the outsized military we have now."

US Economy: Larger Picture

October 17, 2010

A number of pundits have been tip-toeing toward uncomfortable truths about the state of the US economy these days, truths economists have warned about for quite awhile. Unless you've been living in Sleepy Hollow, surrendering entirely to dreams of yesteryear or to Tea Party mythology, you probably understand that the US economy is now a distinct subset of the global economy. We may know this somewhere up there in our heads but we haven't (myself included) really grasped the extent of the implications. Some of us may still believe that up and coming economies out there may beat us in fields like manufacturing, textiles, service centers, and other lower paid professions that require less training, but that we still excel in the fields that generate higher incomes. After all we have Silicon Valley, New Jersey's pharmaceuticals, Wall Street, the best research centers, the best universities—don't we?

It's certainly comfortable to think we're still ahead where it counts; sort of like opium, pipe dreams sooth the rough edges. Comforting until you begin to see or hear about indications that our hold on these advantages is no longer a given. A New York Times editorial recently suggested that others have snuck up on us over the last thirty years while we were complacently spending more than we made, importing way more than we exported. If we are so far ahead, why isn't the total value of what we export greater than the value of what we import? Unfortunately the export/ import discrepancy is a fact not only because we borrowed irresponsibly on housing prices that turned out to be in bubble territory, spending the money on imports; in fact, if that were the whole problem, we could probably rest easy; we're already scaling back our buying and even saving. No, the serious problem is on the export side.[42]

Just how serious the export problem may be struck me when the New York Times editorial, mentioned above, hit on what was once my own field, computer software. The stars of the field used to be US programmers. Back in the 90's, when the small software company I worked for began hiring offshore programmers, I didn't think much of the talent out there in the rest of the world. They could write programs, as long as the specs designed by our home-grown hotshots were clear; seldom did they show anything like productive creativity. Now the Times editorial claims that offshore programmers are likely to be designers with their own strokes of creative genius, their own mastery of the newest technology; and, of course, they are way less expensive. Looks like exporting even such a high end item as home grown software may no longer be without serious, low price competition.

I remember reading a book a couple of years ago (the name and author escape me) that dismissed these trends with the comforting thought that we still control the world's mythology. What they want is American; our life style, our ads, our Hollywood, our heroes are the world's aspirations. I wonder how long that thin reed will anchor our life style. I suspect that once worker's in the emerging nations move up the work hierarchy they may well develop their own sense of pride and their own heroes, leaving ours behind.

---

[42] I do wonder if the terms import and export don't over-simplify inter-dependencies in the new global market. Let's say GE designs a generator in the US and then builds it in China. The finished product is then imported from China back to the US. Certainly part of the expense of production is the design. How much of the design cost is considered a US export, and how much of the finished product is chalked up on the import side as design expense and therefore really made in the U S of A. I'm sure there's an economist out there somewhere who has figured out what import and export now mean (one I haven't read), but I doubt the official statistics reflect any revised insights. We haven't even fully implemented sensible and widely recognized adjustments to inflation figures.

I think we might want to ask what is making the emerging world surge ahead with such energy and such success. Or, we might ask whether, for some reason, our get up and go has gotten up and went. The portion of the emerging world that is surging is in a sweet spot for productivity. They are not so poor that just securing shelter, food, and water absorbs all their energy, but they are not well off, as we have defined well off, either. They are poor enough to hunger for 'better' lives, and most seem to have bought into our notion that a better life means affluence at any cost. They seem willing to invest in the effort, infrastructure, and education that deliver affluence eventually. That drive used to propel our country. Immigrants came here to prosper; students came to get top of the line education. They still do, but we seem determined to throw as many obstacles in the way of immigrants as we can devise, and the students are coming to polish their resumes and then returning home rather than staying and driving the US economy forward.

Meanwhile we seem determined to invest in war and the already affluent.[43] A simple graph in the Newark Star Ledger reveals our priorities. The chart compares three sources of projected debt for the

---

[43] The Newark Star Ledger had a graph showing the share of income gains going to the top 1 percent vs. the bottom 90% of households at various dates in our history. Here's a sample:

1923-1929 bottom 90% = about 17% top 1 % = 70%—Great Depression

1960-1969 bottom 90% = about 65% top 1% = about 11%—It wasn't the economy that led to protests.

1982-1989 bottom 90% = about 25% top 1% = about 40%—Reaganomics shifts income gains solidly to the top. Thanks Gipper. This shift stayed about the same through the Clinton years.

2002-2007 bottom 90% = about 12% top 1% = about 65%—thanks W, trickle down brings us back to depression level inequality. Such top heavy economies don't do all that well, incidentally.

2008-2016???????

And, the current results in terms of actual assets as opposed to income gains? Here's a summary of a chart by blogger Barry Ritholtz as described by Charles Hugh Smith. See—

"Dear "Middle Class" Americans: Most Of You Are Debt Serfs With Zero Assets", Oct. 12, 2010, 11:53 AM "Blog Of Two Minds" By Charles Hugh Smith

decade from 2009-2019. Obama's bailouts and stimulus—1.1 trillion, wars in Afghanistan and Iraq—1.8 trillion, Bush era tax cuts—5.1 trillion. Let's take a look at what this debt buys us. As I mentioned in my previous entry, the bailouts are being paid back with interest. Even AIG, mentioned as one of the serious laggards, is working its way toward paying back. Recent estimates include the encouraging news that we may regain 90% of the TARP outlay; not bad for a program that saved our economic system. Bailing out GM looks like a winner. Sales are up boosting jobs, and at some point even holdouts, who like myself believe that a 12 year old Dodge will be fine as long as it keeps running, will have to consider buying something.

The stimulus? On the whole it has produced jobs. Paul Krugman and others (myself included) would argue that it was way too little, given the seriousness of the recession, but it helped. Now Obama has proposed more help for small business, and even Republicans, who pretend to care about small business, may well have to vote for it to avoid complete hypocrisy. The miniscule portion that is going toward infrastructure comes with the promise to pay back in the same way such long term debt financed projects have paid off in the past. Would anyone like to help me out here by calculating what the TVA or the Interstate Highway System has returned on investment?

And what about the wars; what do they buy us? Several years ago I wrote on the notion that we needed to spend so much blood and money to subdue a fanatic living in a cave. I still find the notion ludicrous. In one of his last Newsweek articles, I was encouraged to read that Fareed Zakaria seems to find our infatuation with this nut case almost as unbalanced on our part as I do. He focused

http://www.businessinsider.com/dear-middle-class-americans-most-of-you-are-debt-serfs-with-zero-assets-2010-10

The first chart depicts total wealth, which includes depreciating assets that are illiquid (SUVs, boats, furniture, etc.) and typically overvalued. In terms of financial wealth, the top 20% own fully 93% of all assets.

If we characterize the top 20% as "wealthy," then the next 20% would be the "upper middle class" (60% -80%) and the third quintile (60% - 40%) would be "middle class." In terms of financial wealth, the Great Middle Class owns a mere 6% of total assets. The bottom 40% (the "working class" and "the poor") own less than 1%.

on the immense expenditures in new security agencies; I tend to wonder why we charged into Iraq to replace Saddam—someone who distrusted Islamic Imams more than we did at the time. Economically, the only advantage either Iraq or Afghanistan has to offer will probably go to China, if they beat us to development of new mineral discoveries in Afghanistan.

The really expensive item, the Bush tax cuts, bought us the worst 10 year economy in our memory. I know this because I've watched my portfolio stagnate for 10 years. My US stock funds didn't even keep up with inflation. My Canada fund proved much better, but then the Bushy trickle-downers didn't have much influence north of the border. A middle class worker, thinking of voting these geniuses back into office, ought to consider their miserly salary gains over the same 10 years. Teachers, firemen, policemen, and government workers who vote Republican this year might consider shooting themselves in the foot as a more productive alternative.

Tax cuts did not reinvigorate the US economy nor did the anemic recovery trickle down. I'd argue that US tax cuts or tax increases are in fact marginal concerns, despite my increase taxes campaign; neither will solve our economic problems. The real issues facing us are much more difficult. Finding ways to exist in a world of other striving and increasingly successful nations will require us to engage the rest of the world in ways we have not felt necessary during the brief period when America seemed to reign.

The Bush era go it alone arrogance needs to be the last gasp of such a pea brained stance. We'll need to become much more attuned to all those international relationships Tea Party types love to denigrate. We need to work with the rest of the world to solve problems like currency manipulation, fair trade practices, money laundering, shady bank accounts, rogue energy companies, global warming, fresh water supplies and hosts of other international problems. To think that we can solve these problems on our own looks more and more like lunacy, popular lunacy, but lunacy none-the-less.

Arab Democracy?

February 19, 2011

Much to my current embarrassment I must now confess to having wondered if Arab Democracy didn't approach oxymoron status. With the exception of Turkey (not primarily Arab), so many countries in the region seemed incapable of anything benevolent in the way of governance other than benign, father-figure monarchies while too many remained straight jacketed by dictatorships and several of those degenerated into mafia like, predatory police states. Why would such a vast region, full of such diversity in culture, natural resources, and circumstances remain so backward looking when it came to their chosen forms of government? It didn't help my thinking that one of my favorite movies, "Lawrence of Arabia", ended with the victorious Arab confederation led by Lawrence making an absolute mess of governing the city they so brilliantly captured.

I was not unaware of the usual liberal excuses for Arab choices. For instance, there's the notion that Anglo dominance of the region, accompanied by the bigotry of low expectations, seeped into their souls and rotted their brains. Or, that we provided military muscle under the guise of aid, and militaries have not exactly shined as beacons of democracy despite apparent belief amongst Egyptians that in their case military influence is on the whole positive. And my favorite excuse, that in the case of oil rich nations those resources and our need for them helped monarchs and dictators buy off discontent. I still believe these influences had an effect, and I still believe that their attitudes toward women will continue to hold them back. But clearly, now, we need to understand that none of these thoughts included any clues that would have helped us comprehend the current Arab revolutions.

In fact, I'd argue that our concepts of the Arab world influenced our own policies as much or more than they influenced Arab countries. Our portrayal of their supposed inadequacies led us to practice a cold and calculated policy toward them that we justified over the many years under a number of telling names—containment, balance of power, real politic—and, since the end of the cold war, strategic interests, narrowly defined as oil and Israel. In my more idealistic years (my wife believes this entry may yet prove that the tendency lingers), I remember writing an editorial, published in the Princeton Packet, which attacked Nixon/Kissinger's balance of power, the worst and most telling of these terms.

Think about that name for a foreign policy—balance of power. Do you see anything in the name that suggests we have any concern for the people or countries we are balancing against each other? Do you see any indication that a war between two neighboring countries, Iraq and Iran, for instance, in which millions died, would matter as long as neither dominated and in doing so altered the balance? It's a chessboard concept in which the power of the key pieces matter, nothing else, and pawns are expendable. In such a world dictatorships are much more manageable than democracies. You can buy them and threaten them with much more predictable results. As long as you don't think about the people or better, suppress them and keep them uninformed, such calculating policies seem to work.

For a nation with a strong belief in its own moral core, we can only hope that our foreign policy, in practice, was more nuanced than the concepts behind 'balance of power' would imply. For instance we trained the younger ranks of the Egyptian military; no small contribution to their positive role. Still, the term balance of power and its policy implications couldn't help but make many of us in this country uncomfortable, and we shouldn't be surprised if large portions of the Arab public took us at our word. Uncomfortable we were, but fear of the Soviet Union and our attitudes toward what we allowed ourselves to view as 'less advanced cultures', like all Arabs in general, allowed us to overlook the obvious clash between our values and our stated policy.

We need a new name for what we stand for in the world, and we need to purge whatever balance of power concepts still muddy our approach and our message. We have no excuse now for having anything to do with such a bankrupt foreign policy concept. No need to balance Soviet military power. The Soviet Union imploded, as any advocate of competitive markets should have understood it would. And, we now know that the Arab peoples, we (me included) too willingly dismissed, have a moral core capable of mirroring the best in us.

So, why don't we consider a foreign policy that recognizes this new reality, named, perhaps, 'people politics' or 'information politics'? Why don't we take on a really simple position? We believe in democracies and in the people's right to know and based on that knowledge to control their own countries. And, we will seek to advocate for and support people who demonstrate their belief in these values we cherish, often by putting their lives on the line for those values. Wouldn't such a stance make you feel more comfortable? I would feel great relief.

Nice thoughts, you say, but how do we support such nebulous concepts? A Times editorial last week, now in the recycle somewhere[44], gave a perfect, concrete example. Take a portion, not even the major portion, of our military aid to Egypt ($1.3 billion/year?) and direct it instead to building 20 schools throughout Egypt, as our gift of thanks to the Egyptian people. In one stroke we would be saying that we respect the minds of your youth that brought us this transforming spirit, and we recognize that what you have revealed to us within yourselves makes the level of military aid we now supply less necessary. Why can't our government, and yes, our president, be bold enough to seize the moment by making such a concrete statement of America's new awareness,

---

[44] Saved by a letter to the editor. The article was by Thomas L. Friedman "Pharaoh without a Mummy", 2/16/2011.

now? We might add that shutting down the Internet is shutting down a major conduit for knowledge and that we consider such actions an affront to progress.

We need to keep in mind how stark a contrast such a new direction might seem to many in the Arab world after too many years of our own complicity in the old world order, in one man rule governments, and in reliance on military solutions. There are even darker sides to our image. Abu Ghraib, torture, rendition, rendition to Egypt no less, we sent people into the hands of the very torturers Egyptians so clearly reject; we have a lot of black marks against our name in the Arab world. If we really care about what they think or about whom we are, we would begin serious investigations into these horrendous actions by our government. I don't see our country shouldering this responsibility to call to account the torturers amongst us anytime soon, so in the meantime let's at least support those in the Arab world showing us the way.

We are not incapable of providing such support. Already the discussion of military intervention in the affairs of Arab countries has come around from 'let's charge right in' (Wolfowitz, Pearle, Chaney and the rest of the preemption gang) to maybe military solutions have limited value. Leaders in this change have come most resoundingly from the military itself. Where we are engaged we hear much more about building infrastructure and winning support from the people than we hear about body counts (the old Vietnam measure of success). Recently our military leaders, especially Secretary of Defense Robert Gates, have suggested that military personnel reductions may be possible. That's a welcome indication of sanity, and maybe it means we are getting ready for the next step. Maybe we can cut our military budget to ½ what the rest of the world spends and really address our debt.

And, here's something encouraging; congressional members of the Tea Party joined with liberals recently to eliminate what's called the alternate jet engine for the F-35 fighter. Maybe they can even get together and scrap 1000 or so of the jets themselves out of the planned force of 2400 projected for purchase over the next 25 years.[45] Say, some of the $380 billion the full complement would cost, according to the usual under-estimates, might go to something more in line with our new strategic thinking, a few thousand hospitals or schools, perhaps.

But wait, I get ahead of where we are. The Tea Party members who voted to scrap the alternate engine did not represent districts in Ohio and Indiana where the engine is built. All nine of these freshman tea party representatives did what congressmen do traditionally, voted local interests over national interests. Breaks from the past way of doing business, so much a part of the Tea Party hoopla, will have to measure up better than this example, if we really intend to bring about change.

I can imagine a simple spreadsheet that would provide some sense of whether we are really capable of changing our own democracy. Take each congressman's voting record on budget items and correlate the votes with whether the money spent goes to his or her district. Where the money does not go to their district, give them a pass. Maybe they were thinking of the country rather than themselves. Where the money goes to his or her district, give them a question mark requiring further investigation. I'm hoping that someone who doesn't need to bring in the firewood right now will take up this task. Or, maybe real news organizations like the NY Times or PBS will take it on. Just this one task done well might make the federal cuts to PBS funding look like the bad bargain they surely are in this, the information age.

---

[45] Here's an update. Leon Panetta, new Secretary of Defence is reported to have said to be considering reductions or delays in the production of this new jet.
New York Times Article, November 7, 2011, 'Panetta Weighs Pentagon Cuts Once Off Limits'.

CHAPTER 5
Middle Class Revival

Introduction

November, 2011

Anyone who has had the TV tuned into a news program, read a paper, opened up a news site on the internet, or talked to their barber recently knows that the middle class has stagnated over the last 10 to 30 years while the ultra-rich have gobbled up income and assets at astonishing rates. The figures are incontrovertible, and liberals or progressives, including me, cannot help but cite these figures with warnings that they signal problems for our country's financial, social, and spiritual health.

Republicans and conservatives in general respond by extolling the upward mobility that has been the mark of American society since our beginnings as a nation. They see any attempt to redistribute wealth as an insistence on 'equality of outcome' as opposed to 'equality of opportunity', as Paul Ryan stated in a recent speech entitled "Saving the American Idea". They derive their position in part from Ayn Rand, Paul Ryan's guru, who, in <u>Atlas Shrugged,</u> attacks the morally repugnant demands of the needy as opposed to the virtues of risk taking, creative, and courageous entrepreneurs. Ayn Rand may have had reason to fight against the Marxist notion—from each according to his ability to each according to his need. But, I fail see why conservatives continue to harp on last century's battles.

What troubles me about my own position in this argument is that the statistics on income and assets I love to quote emphasize the 'outcome' conservatives love to attack. I still believe the outcome has the potential to distort our society, as I argue in this chapter. But, as a Newark Star Ledger editorial[46] makes clear, the

---

[46] 'Newark Star Ledger', November 6, 2011, editorial

real weakness in the conservative position is on the equality of opportunity side. Conservatives oppose Pell Grants that give those without funds the opportunity for better outcomes. They oppose union organizing and the minimum wage, America's attempts to give a boost to those who work hard to achieve better outcomes.

Not mentioned in the Newark Ledger editorial, but a favorite argument of mine, is that conservatives constantly attack the inheritance tax. One has to ask why the children of 'virtuous, risk taking entrepreneurs' need all the advantages they can garnish from oddles of inherited money, while those without such advantages do not deserve a boost like a Pell Grant or a decent minimum wage or the right to organize.

Inconceivable

January 24, 2011

Back in early May, 2008, when, in a discouraged moment, I thought Republicans had a chance of winning the 2008 election, I wrote an entry entitled 'Why Do Republicans Ever Win?' Now in 2011, after they actually did win, I'm even more baffled. After just two years of Democratic initiatives, we Democrats are back on the defensive, trying to defend a humane healthcare bill, a brilliantly successful execution of TARP (even AIG seems to be paying back with a profit for the government), an inadequate but at least well intentioned stimulus, small business aid, financial regulation, the end of 'don't ask, don't tell', an arms control treaty with Russia, and a number of other realistic and forward looking accomplishments.

We are defending these accomplishments against a party that still believes in trickle-down economics, continues to support tax reductions for those who need them least, believes in supporting a bloated American military (except for Rand Paul), tends to use our military power unwisely, and fails to support many of those willing to give their lives for our country by failing to support enthusiastically the end of 'don't ask, don't tell' and by failing to support the Dream Act at all. Again, I find myself asking, why does such a backward looking party ever win?

Well, now, those paragraphs felt good. Every once in a while it helps to clear the bile ducts by adopting what I like to call my Bob Herbert 'tell it like you feel it' stance. Bob Herbert, himself, let go recently (as he often does) in his December 28, NY Times editorial. Here's a sample:

What we're really seeing is an erosion of standards of living for an enormous portion of the population, including a substantial segment of the once solid middle class.

Not only is this not being addressed, but the self-serving, right-ward lurch in Washington is all but guaranteed to make matters worse for working people. The zealots reading the economic tea leaves see brighter days ahead. They can afford to be sanguine. They're working.

On the very same editorial page, David Brooks, who often challenges my intellect as opposed to clearing my bile ducts, described several essays he chose as the best of the year. Here's his summary of Charlie LeDuff's essay about Detroit "Who Killed Aiyana Stanley Jones":

...a city in which 80 percent of eighth graders are unable to do basic math, the crime lab was closed because of ineptitude, 500 fires are set every month, and 50 percent of the drivers are operating without a license.

And here's his summary of Tyler Cowen's "The Inequality That Matters":

Smart people, especially in the financial sector, now have tremendous incentives to take great risks. If the risks fail, they still have millions in the bank. If the risks pay off, they get enormously rich. The result is a society with more inequality and more financial instability.

I couldn't help noting that both Herbert and Brooks seemed to find the same basic issue central. We have a financial community out of control and very rich, playing the rest of the country like a fiddle; and we have a decaying middle class, as well as the out-and-out impoverished, dropping off our radar. And yet, we end up electing Republicans whose major contribution over the last twelve years has been preserving the Bush tax cuts for the wealthy while failing to fund two wars. Why do we do this? I've struggled with this question for years, and I've ended up deciding that there are many answers.

Back in 2008, I was intrigued by the notion of cues that associated a candidate with a large segment of the voting population. Reagan could mention welfare queens, and a significant portion of the population knew he meant blacks and they were happy to attack blacks without having to say they were attacking blacks or poor whites or anyone unlike themselves. But cues are much more subtle than that. In a celebrity obsessed culture, just associating with a star personality can identify a candidate as one of us, if we happen to be a fan; and being one of us is much more powerful than any position or argument. Sarah Palin shoots and hunts; for far too many, that's good enough; no need to know if she thinks. In fact, that she is not associated with people who believe in sustained thought—intellectual elitists, scientists, and the like—endears her to millions.

Recently I tried to figure out if various American myths were the driving forces behind voting decisions. Large portions of the public respond to any appeal echoing the Horatio Alger myth that one's own efforts are the only determinates of success despite clear evidence that social position, the wealth of one's parents, luck, and other advantages so often play a part. The myth puts any progressive program at an initial disadvantage that is hard to overcome. It is easier to dismiss financially unsuccessful people as lazy or lacking in initiative, especially if you believe their condition is entirely their fault, than to think through progressive programs that might help even the playing field by redressing societal imbalances.

Republicans are particularly adept at dismissing or even attacking large portions of the public without paying a political price. They attack any organization that might support workers; unions for example. How dare workers organize for their own benefit[47]? They attack government workers. How dare they unite in an effort to do as well as or even better than their stagnating, privately employed counterparts? There's good evidence that

---

[47] Note that the United Auto Workers have taken over responsibility for retirees' medical insurance relieving the companies of a $1500/vehicle expense so the companies could better compete. There were other concessions too. Seeing a financial issue, unions responded intelligently by sacrificing; Republicans, well, I'd really like to see them think out of their boxes more often, like the unions have.

public employees don't do better[48], but evidence is not relevant when mounting a generalization. This sort of non-specific attack on groups is like negative campaigning against individuals; and, despite our protestations to the contrary, we all know negative campaigning works. We can label Republicans as the party of 'no', but as I've argued before, 'no' beats 'yes' consistently at the gut level and then at the polls.

Republicans reserve their most consistent negative attack for government itself. Small government and less spending make up the mantra—a fundamental, almost religious belief. The great moral weakness of America, they would have us believe these days, is passing on impossible to manage government debt to our children. Passing on polluted rivers and oceans, man-made global warming[49], a crumbling infrastructure, a struggling educational system, a fossil fuel dependent economy, an over-sized military industrial complex, a moneyed aristocracy and working peasantry—for Republicans it would seem that none of these other dangers we may well leave behind compare to the fiscal/mon-

---

[48] Newark Star Ledger, May 17,2010 by columnist Bob Braun reporting on work done by Jeffery Keefe, an associate professor at Rutgers' School of Management and Labor Relations, Economist William Rodgers also from Rutgers, and Carl Van Horn, another professor just appointed to the state's Council on Economic Advisors by Gov. Chris Christie.
See http://blog.nj.com/njv_bob_braun/2010/05/rutgers_studies_public_versus.html Public and private sector jobs need to be compared on the basis of similar educational level, experience and work schedule. When the comparisons are done with these controls in place, private compensation beats public compensation both in terms of salaries and overall compensation, according to this Rutgers study.
[49] The NY Times (Dec. 22, 2010) had one of the most convincing articles I've read on man-made global warming. The article described 50 years of careful CO_2 records kept by Dr. Charles Keeling and his son. The long term CO_2 records gleaned from polar ice drillings show that CO_2 variations in the atmosphere varied over the ages from 200-300 parts per million. The Keeling records show that we are now approaching a never before extreme of 400 parts per million. Also the CO_2 variations track the ice ages—higher numbers, less ice, greater warming. Instead of dismissing man-made global warming we need to hear more intelligent public discussion. Then we need to act. My own Republican congressman voted for the House cap and trade bill. Reason can prevail; thoughtful Republicans can think out of the box.

etary disaster they so willingly predict. Their anguish increases whenever the need for government stimulus spending and debt increases, as it did during the most recent crisis.

Of course the debt needs to be addressed, but not in the way most Republicans advocate. The various commissions that have reported back advise a mix of tax increases and spending cuts. The commissions agree on a phased in approach so as not to do damage to what is still a weak recovery. They face head on the real issues of debt built into Social Security, Medicare, Medicaid, and the military. Unlike too many Republicans, the commissioners do not harp endlessly on discretionary spending and they do not harp endlessly on waste and fraud. Certainly by now we have enough evidence that our debt problem is what the commissioners have identified and not the easy targets too many Republicans prefer to address.

So how should we proceed? Let's first admit that strong government is essential to a free society and a free market economy. Without law there is no freedom, without effective regulation and well conceived trade agreements there is no free market economy. Law, regulation, and trade agreements are the province of government. Surely we all know this. We are disagreeing on how much government we are willing to accept and fund, or we are disagreeing on which level of government—federal, state, county or local—should perform the necessary functions.

I'd argue that trade agreements belong entirely to the federal government and the constitution would agree[50]. Regulation, well, unless you want a patch work quilt of regulations for each regulated activity, then chose federal regulation. Of course we often leave regulations like zoning and environmental regulation to state, county or local entities, and I have only relatively minor

---

[50] See Article 1 Section 8. Federalist paper number 42 connects regulation of foreign trade with the interstate commerce clause, arguing that you cannot have one without the other. Too bad Congress limited itself to reading a badly edited version of the constitution. They'd all benefit from a reading of the Federalist papers too.

quibbles here and there with that arrangement. Law is confusing beyond what I could possibly discuss here, but the constitution is quite clear on the ultimate authority, and that authority is federal.

A strong federal government is fundamental to our democracy, and I would argue that we are weakening ours by under-funding the discretionary portion of the federal government's budget, the same portion Republicans mistakenly target for further reductions. They are mistaken not only because discretionary spending has little to do with the long term deficit, as the commissions have made clear, but because our democracy needs more of what this portion of the budget provides.

I have only incidental evidence to support such a broad contention. Inspectors can't make more than cursory inspections of meat packing plants (forget spinach), oil rigs go far too long without oversight[51], park rangers risk their lives to an unnecessary degree because they lack adequate backup, border guards and airport security personnel are undertrained or underpaid[52] or both, our legal system can't provide sufficient council for the indigent or keep up with case loads, nuclear plants lack adequate security, ships enter our ports with tons of uninspected cargo, infrastructure crumbles—the list is long.

Of course there is room for greater efficiency in performing some of the functions budgeted under discretionary funding. My favorite example is the agency responsible for providing

---

[51] Republicans are already gearing up to oppose any implementation or funding of regulations based on the recently released report by the commission set up by the president to investigate the gulf oil spill. Environmentalists should be encouraged to see that the EPA (silenced by the Bush administration) is back doing its job. It recently revoked a mountaintop mining permit for a West Virginia coal mine based on the clean water act. They cited science, the opposition (Democratic incidentally) cited jobs. Again citing science, the EPA ruled that PCB's in a landfill were not at sufficient levels to cause birth defects in surrounding towns and therefore expansion of the landfill could proceed. I would be encouraged, as one concerned with environmental issues, to see our politicians cite the science behind their environmental decisions, along with whatever other concerns might be driving those decisions.

[52] $32,000/year for a border guard. I have trouble seeing that as adequate let alone overpaid.

law enforcement with information on guns used in crimes. This agency still works with paper, and therefore they employ more personnel than they need. Why do I like this example of inefficiency so much? The NRA threatens any congressman that might turn this job into a computerized operation, and I don't care much for NRA politics. We could probably save a couple of million by improving this obvious target; but, obvious as it is, frightened politicians can't get past the NRA, and those politicians include, to my embarrassment, Democrats, though they tend to be Republican.

We can save discretionary spending funds here and there, and we should; but let's stop the distractions and the symbolism (like the 35 million dollar reduction for financing the congress) and begin talking about the real problem. Secretary of Defense, Gates, made a start by eliminating or scaling back a few unnecessary military hardware projects and by suggesting that army and marine troops could be cut as the two current wars wind down. He even mentioned that financial concerns required military cutbacks. That's an unheard of thought in most Republican circles. They tend toward leaving this 800 pound (ok $700 billion/year) gorilla out of their calculations. Let's hope they can manage to save the money pouring into the two ongoing wars, once we pull out, without starting a couple more unfunded conflicts.

Gates at least made a start. But, he barely began the discussion I believe we need to have about the function of our military in the 21st Century. His comment about fiscal constraints on the military at least provides an opening. But, as I mentioned in a previous entry, we need to listen to an odd pair, Libertarian Rand Paul and progressive Barney Frank, to get at the real question. What ought to be the military's mission in the world we inhabit today?

On this subject, Gates' recent statements sound like cold war thinking to me. Do we really need to continue to be the world's policeman, or perhaps could we share this function a lot more? Do we need to build nations out of tribal cultures, crush brutish dictators, protect our Asian allies from China, or could we emphasize other approaches than military and ask for some more real help from others? Do we really believe our military can move the moral center of the world toward freedom, or do we let our example of freedom and civility[53] speak for us and then wait for the world to move that way itself?

If we readjust our views on these more fundamental questions about what our military should or should not do in the future, I suspect we could reduce the military budget by $100 billion or so a year starting slowly now and escalating the reductions as the wars wind down. I don't know, maybe we set a goal of $400 billion per year by 2016. That military budget would still dwarf any other in the world.[54] $400 billion should be enough to defend our country and provide more than our fair share of global needs. Some of those savings should go to real deficit reduction; some should go to another GI bill, so returning troops can gain skills needed to become productive civilians rather than burdening an already shaky labor market; and some will need to be set aside for the medical needs of the retuning troops, which we know will be significant.

Of the other major deficit generators—Social Security, Medicare, and Medicaid—Social Security is a breeze compared to the other two. Republicans need to consider a slight hike in the payroll tax and Democrats need to consider slight adjustments to the age requirements. We've done these adjustments in the past and we can do them again. The only real objections to age adjustments have to do with the type of labor people do. In general, physically demanding labor wears people out earlier than office work,

---

[53] Civility? I keep trying. The president's speech at the Tucson memorial service should inspire us all to try harder. I've edited this entry with his thoughts in mind.

[54] Here are the percentages for global military spending (2009) as printed in the Newark Star Ledger—source: Whitehouse.gov. US—46.5%, China—6.6%, France—4.2%, U.K.—3.8%, Russia—3.2%, Next 10 countries—20.7%, rest—14.7%. US spending in inflation adjusted dollars decreased and then leveled during the Clinton years and then shot up from around $300 billion in 2000 to around $600 billion in 2008. Unfortunately that trajectory continues. Eisenhower's farewell warnings about the military-industrial complex still have meaning.

though I know of one farmer who worked because he wanted to well into his 70's. My own thought on this issue would be to consider adjustments to the disability requirements built into Social Security, but I haven't thought enough yet to figure out how that might work.

The problems with Medicare and Medicaid deficits are multi-layered and far from simple. I'll limit myself here to considering the bottom layer—the escalating costs of medical care itself. Medical care costs keep increasing at a rate much greater than mere inflation. Some provisions in the Healthcare bill (Patient Protection and Afford-able Care Act[55]—H.R. 3590) attempt to deal with this part of the problem. You can take a look at a good summary of what is in the act by looking at the Congressional Budget Office (CBO) summary, in a 21 page letter to Senate majority leader, Harry Reid. You will see a number of items there designed to reduce underlying medical costs. [56]

The focus of the letter is the CBO estimate of how the bill will affect the deficit from 2010-2019. The CBO estimates that the bill will decrease the deficit by 143 billion over that time period. No attempt is made to deal with any of the savings from more widespread primary care like fewer people waiting until they need much more expensive advanced or even emergency room care. As with any estimate it is easy to quibble with many parts of it; and, as I would expect, Republicans discard it, seldom bothering to discuss details.

CNN's Dr. Gupta attempted to pin down Republican Congressman and medical doctor Tom Price recently and made little progress. Tom Price simply asserted that the bill would increase

---

[55] Isn't that a catchy title? Democrats could learn at least one lesson from Republicans. Make the language work for us rather than against us. I will soldier on, though, and never call the act anything else, if I can manage to remember that name more than 5 minutes. OK, I shortened it to Healthcare bill.

[56] See Go to http://www.cbo.gov Letter to Harry Reid, December 19, 2009. Index 10868. This letter refers to the 'manager's amendment' and references a November 18, 2009 analysis of the Patient Protection and Affordable Care Act as originally proposed.

costs, decrease care and the quality of care, decrease Health Savings Accounts, damage Advantage Plans, and restrict coverage choice. After agreeing with almost every serious commentator that the status quo prior to passage of the Healthcare bill was unsustainable, Congressman Price offered old Republican alternative bills.

During the Healthcare debate of 2009 Republicans offered various alternative bills.[57] I've read and commented on HR3970 (2/1/2010 blog), and I still think, as I did then, that it offers little of value. It has only one exclusively Republican approach to reducing underlying costs, and that's tort reform. As I argued, tort reform savings are difficult to estimate. Those who have made the effort put the cost at from 2% to 5% of overall medical costs, depending on how much is allowed for CYA procedures that would not be necessary if the threat of a lawsuit didn't encourage them. The estimates include the premium costs of medical malpractice insurance. 2% to 5% would not be insignificant if the Republican bill could recoup a good portion of this cost. But, mercifully, it doesn't attempt to. The bill allows for compensatory as well as punitive damages, though it does attempt to limit lawyer profit on the patient's side (but not on the medical practitioner's side).

Tort reform might be worth a look, but there are better ways to handle malpractice. As I've discussed before, Kaiser Permanente and a number of other large medical providers establish best practices for all medical procedures and then adjust and review those procedures as the need arises. No doctor can possibly keep up with every medical change that comes along; some common attempt is clearly necessary. 'Best practices' has the advantage over malpractice reform mainly because it addresses the issues of how to deal with medical conditions before a disaster rather than after. But, it also provides doctors with a line of defense if a malpractice case does arise. There's no need to order unnecessary

---

[57] Affordable Care, Health Care Freedom, Empowering Patients First, Patients Choice—better titles at least.

and expensive diagnostic procedures in order to build a possible defense if you've followed recognized best practices.

The real question about establishing 'best practices' is just how restrictive the guidelines might become on the judgment calls physicians make when dealing with individual cases day in and day out. Republicans are right to worry about this issue, but wrong to move too quickly toward labeling any government effort toward establishing best practices as bureaucrats getting between doctor and patient. Guidelines that remain guidelines do not restrict in the same way that rules with penalties would, for instance. Funding an independent body, to study best practices, would be even less intrusive. There are fine line distinctions to be made here, exactly the kind of problem labels so grossly distort. We should not forget that without official guidelines we leave these decisions far too open to insurance company influence, based on the profit motive, not medically sound science.

Kaiser Permanente established a peer review procedure for cases in which doctors felt that a particular patient's situation required departure from the guidelines. Reviews of this sort allow doctors to think through difficult cases with colleagues. Also I would think review would provide yet another line of defense in malpractice cases. Kaiser Permanente pays for any malpractice litigation or claims itself, without resorting to insurance companies; yet another approach for larger medical providers.

Republican bills contain a number of other potentially reasonable provisions. They advocate investment in preventive care and supplemental health insurance for low income families—reasonable proposals. There's a provision to provide tax credits to citizens not retired or on Medicare, $2,300 ($5,700 for families) to supplement purchase of individual insurance policies. Except for preventive care, I don't see much that will reduce the costs of Medicare or Medicaid, though. And, I don't find much in the Republican plans that isn't better handled in the plan that passed. We should be working to improve the bill we have.

Once Republicans get serious and admit that the way is forward not backward, I'll try to listen harder to what they have to say. They need to understand that the notion of a single superpower is getting as old as so many of their other positions; and not incidentally, maintaining our belief that we need to remain as the only superpower is becoming a far too expensive fantasy. The 21st Century will have a number of power centers that will require complex and carefully considered international cooperation with ideas generated from multiple cultural backgrounds. As one of those power centers, we need to address our own problems, and if we do our influence will be significant. Even our own problems with an aging population and greater Social Security and Medicare needs are not ours alone. Others—Japan, China, and the European Union—are worse off in terms of the number of young workers supporting such programs vs. the number who will need those services. We have lots to do, our federal government has lots to do, simple slogans and set ideas will not help us move forward.

Solidarity Forever

April 8, 2011

As a progressive there is not much question about where I stand on union bargaining rights. My stand is quite simple, workers have the right to organize and magnify the effect of their demands by bargaining collectively rather than as individuals, whether they are public or private employees. Over a hundred years of union struggle, waged against the overwhelming power of industrial and financial giants as well as government powers, went into securing that right. And, they are not responsible if the other side in the bargaining process fails to bargain effectively or promises, in legitimate negotiations, what they cannot deliver.

I take this position even though I have never been a union member. I've been a union onlooker from afar; throughout my career, no institution or company I ever worked for had a union workforce. My father was not a union member[58]; as far as I know, no one I knew as a youth had a father in the union. Not being personally involved, however, does not mean my attachment to the cause lacks passion; my attachment is decidedly not simply intellectual. How could it be when I shared so passionately in the protest movements of the '60's? Our music was based on union music from Woody Guthrie to Pete Seeger to Bob Dylan and Joan Baez; we felt the power of union songs. We admired and attempted to emulate their solidarity in our own acts of protest.

---

[58] I make this claim despite the following contradictory evidence provided by a long time friend.

My Daddy was a Miner
And I'm a Miner's son.
And I'll stick by the Union
Until the job is done.

147

So, when I first heard about Governor Walker's attempt to link Wisconsin's budget issues with the 'evils' of collective bargaining, I had trouble even thinking about whatever his position might have been. I naturally enough assumed that it was a typical political ploy to attack the other party's base, to attack the last middle class bastion now that industrial unions had been weakened by a global workforce and by a government that managed to foist off the Taft-Hartley act as a right to work act, despite Truman's veto. That regressive, pre-McCarthy act required that union leaders sign non-communist affidavits and prohibited a number of union tactics that had helped strengthen their negotiating effectiveness. The right to work laws set in motion by Taft-Hartley led states to outlaw open union shops (closed union shops outlawed altogether); interestingly enough most of the former slave states did so, but not progressive Wisconsin and not my home state, New Jersey.

When I then heard that Walker himself had gone part way toward creating the budget deficit by reducing state business taxes even though Wisconsin's business taxes were not at all out of line, I could only think that 'there they go again trying to palm off trickle-down economics after years of flow up results'. Then to top it off, I learned that unions had made significant concessions in terms of benefits before Governor Walker decided he had his chance to gut them more permanently. Add in the fact that police and firemen unions who supported him were left out of his union busting measures, for the time being anyway, and I was more than convinced that we were dealing with a typical Republican politician who had no problem twisting the facts to fit Republican philosophy and the tactics to fit his own political ambitions. Those union members who think their time will not come should take a look at a really stingy provision being considered by national House Republicans. It denies food stamps to any family that includes a worker on strike. See NY Times Editorial 3/25/11.

It's too bad for my comfort level that I didn't just write this entry then. Instead I started arguing with a member of the next generation. He has no contact with unions actual or emotional. His music was something else, not union at all, except what he may have heard from old folks. I don't think he ever participated in a demonstration. And yet, he had what I had to admit might well be legitimate concerns about whether Wisconsin or other states in trouble could possibly afford the benefits already promised, let alone future benefits. I had to admit that I was not sufficiently informed about the details of what those expenses might be and whether we here in New Jersey could afford our own insufficiently funded pensions or not. Certainly my information on what Wisconsin could afford was sketchy to say the least.

Given my lack of information and my suspicion that any information I could find might well be slanted, I decided to approach the problem in New Jersey by considering what Republicans seem to be (at least these days) constitutionally incapable of considering. I wanted to figure out just what sort of tax increases could at least soften the blow to union jobs and rights in my state. Then I thought that I'd consider just what cuts or adjustments in expenditures I think unions might do well to consider. I figured that the politicians probably wouldn't do any better than I could on my own, so why not give it a try.

I started by accepting Governor Christie's figure for the budget deficit, though accepting anything he says is questionable, as a number of recent articles have pointed out. His prediction for the 2011 budget deficit is $10.7 billion. It's a big number, and as far as I can figure increasing taxes will not cover it all. To place the burden on government workers only is not the answer either. Some combination of tax increases and union cooperation is the fair way to go.

In 2004 and 2009 New Jersey increased income taxes on high wage earners[59]. Why not improve on those measures and establish three high income levels at $250,000, $500,000, and $1,000,000 per annum.

[59] See Center on Budget and Policy Priorities, 'Raising State Income Taxes on High-Income Taxpayers' By Elizabeth McNichol, Andrew Nicholas and Jon Shure·

New Jersey raised its top rate in 2004 to 8.97 percent on taxable income greater than $500,000 (married or single). The previous top rate had been 6.37 percent on income greater than $150,000 for married filing jointly and $75,000 for singles. In 2009, New Jersey temporarily increased income taxes on households with incomes above $400,000. For one year, the tax rate on joint filers with incomes between $400,000 and $500,000 will rise to 8 percent from 6.37; the rate on income between $500,000 and $1 million will increase to 10.25 percent from 8.97 percent; and a new

Dropping down to the $250,000 from the $400,000 or $500,000 Levels of 2004 and 2009 picks up a lot more high income tax payers. If we add these new high income earners to the rapidly increasing numbers earning the two highest brackets, we should see a considerable increase in state revenue. Note that someone earning $250,000 or more pays the increased rate only on any earnings between $250,000 and $500,000 and so on up the ladder. How about a 1% increase above $250,000, a 2% increase above $500,000, and a 3% increase above $1,000,000. We'll call it 1, 2, 3 go for a balanced budget.

Compared to a teacher losing a job, the sacrifice these 1, 2, 3'ers will make seems minimal to me, though of course Republicans will lobby to get rid of the teachers instead. A High School Teacher's salary in New Jersey ranges from $42,742-$59,091 according to payscale. com.[60] Here's a chart indicating just how much more tax surcharges would cost someone making $700,000 a year.[61] You'll need to double the surcharge for my proposal. Note that the chart includes Taxpayer 'A' making just a bit less than the low end of the teacher scale.

High Income Surcharge (1%) on taxpayers with Income over $500,000

	Tax Payer A	Tax Payer B
Income	$40,000	$700,000
Current tax	$1,600	$41,200
Additional tax:		
Income over $500,000	0	$200,000
Times .01=surcharge	0	$2,000
Total tax surcharged	1,600	$43,200

10.75 percent rate is applied to all income over $1 million. These changes will generate about $1 billion in fiscal 2010.

[60]http://www.payscale.com/research/US/Job=High_School_Teacher/Salary/by_ State

[61] op. cit. Elizabeth McNichol, Andrew Nicholas and Jon Shure.

I see the usual Republican objections to increased taxes on the high income earners as little more than smoke and mirrors. They argue that, if we tax high income earners, even a percentage point or so more in income tax, they will leave the state in significant numbers. Republicans even argue that the number of these migrations would be significant enough to seriously counter any proposed revenue gains from the new taxes. That's not only nonsense on the face of it, it's not supported by what happened after the 2004 increase[62] (figures not available for 2009).

Imagine for a minute that you are in one of those three high income brackets. You probably have a high paying job (or a platinum spoon), likely as not in the financial industry or here in NJ in the pharmaceutical industry. You own a home or two and you have a cushy low interest mortgage—5% fixed, say, if you haven't refinanced lately. In the upper two proposed brackets you probably keep the mortgage, primarily because you figure you can make more in the stock market by investing your superfluous cash than you would lose by paying the interest on the loan. So, Republicans argue that, financially sophisticated guy or gal that you are, you are going to sell your home into a depressed real estate market, leave the company paying you handsomely, leave your network of family and friends behind, take your kids out of some of the best schools in the country and move where? Perhaps you'll pick one of those low or no income tax, southern states with lousy schools and few jobs, fewer still in the financial

---

[62] op. cit. Elizabeth McNichol, Andrew Nicholas and Jon Shure

For example, a September 2008 Princeton University study concluded, "the 'half-millionaire tax,' at least in New Jersey, appears to be an effective and efficient revenue-generation mechanism, having little impact on migration patterns among half-millionaire households." The study estimated that New Jersey lost $37.7 million a year from people leaving the state because of the 2004 tax increase. They called this "a small opportunity cost of a tax policy that generated more than $1 billion for Tax Year 2006." Furthermore, the study found that household income has grown rapidly among wealthy New Jerseyans in recent years despite the tax. From 2002 to 2006, the number of New Jersey households with incomes of $500,000 or more grew to 44,000 from 26,000, an increase of 70 percent.

or pharmaceutical industries. And, you will make all these changes to save a few bucks on your state income taxes?

Sometimes I wish for a better argument from Republicans than this high income flight from taxes fantasy so we could seriously move the discussion along. The only 'factual support' I've seen for their position on high income migration takes the total migration numbers out of NJ as an indication of what the high rollers would do. That is smoke. Republicans do better on the face of it when they argue that small business owners often record their business income as personal income. It seems more sensible to think that, if small business owners do that, then raising income taxes on them might cause them to shrink their business investment, and, if they did so, job loses might result.

Some small business owners probably would follow the pattern that Republicans imply would be so damaging to the job market. Those who look at the actual results of increased taxes on such individuals make the following counter points. Compared to the numbers making big money elsewhere, businessmen who file their business income as individuals are few, something like 2 or 3 % of the total with incomes in the proposed top three brackets. For some businessmen, the business is not of the sort that generates jobs. Estate management by survivors, as the estate is being resolved, qualifies as a business for income tax purposes, but it doesn't produce jobs. Partnerships where the partners are not involved in any business decisions also qualify as business participants.[63] Somehow (it's not easy) these 'business men and women'

---

[63] See 'Would Ending Bush's Tax Cuts Hurt Small Business?'—Bloomberg Business Week.
http://www.businessweek.com/magazine/content/10_40/b4197030541676.htm
This debate was triggered by the debate over rescinding the Bush tax cuts that were scheduled to end in 2010. Finding figures specifically for New Jersey has eluded me. Here's the article's conclusion:
The nonpartisan Congressional Research Service, which analyzes issues for lawmakers, largely agreed with Obama in a Sept. 3 report that considered only taxpayers with employees. Its conclusion: Small businesses with actual workers would pay only about 12 percent of the higher taxes.

must be separated from those who actually can make decisions that would affect employment in the calculations that lead to the 2 to 3% figure.

Let's go ahead and assume that the 2 or 3% figure of those making enough to qualify for the high income tax brackets who are business men or women correctly excludes those who have no impact on employment. That means 97 to 98% of those in the high income brackets are not small business owners making the sort of decisions that directly affect job creation. Wouldn't you think that Republican strategists could come up with a more accurately directed policy, if their goal was really small business job preservation? Of course they could. They could make it real simple and give a tax break for each job created. Or, they could stop attacking the 'Affordable Care Act' with its tax credits and other advantages for small business owners. But they don't. Could it be that they really don't care as much about job creation as they do about wealth preservation? If so, pushed to defend wealth preservation, they are forced to fall back on trickle-down economics, a notion so full of nonsense that I give up arguing with anyone who considers it a viable notion. I tend to mock it as the Gadaffi principle. Give me all the money and all the power, and I'll do right by my loving subjects; I promise.

Union members have every reason to reject Republican assertions that tax increases on the wealthy are not part of the solution, and the rest of us should reject that notion too. But union members and, in particular, members of public unions need to rethink some of their own long held beliefs, if state budget deficits are to be controlled. Tax increases can only do so much. I'd ask them to start by thinking about pensions quite broadly. I'd ask them to consider the possibility that pensions are a really bad idea for them as well as for state budgets.

Pensions put decision making in unsteady hands with little incentive for responsible accounting. New Jersey's pension fund, currently valued at $70 billion, has a shortfall of $54 billion.

Politicians, with their eyes on the next election, just love to short change those pension funds or to encourage overestimates of fund returns in order to fill other holes in projected budgets. Robbing pension funds or inflating their potential earnings is less obvious and more popular than increasing taxes. And, it's a big pot of money, much of which won't go out to workers until after voters forget who did what or the politicians move on to something else. Pension juggling is a New Jersey tradition which is why our pension funds are among the most underfinanced in the country.[64] Government workers shouldn't risk trusting pension funds or those who are entrusted with maintaining them.

If they do trust those pension funds, then they are likely to hang around for the payoff. Hanging around in one job is what previous generations did, previous even to mine. I never stayed at one job long enough to collect a 10 year pin. As my interests changed or my talents developed or companies 'let me go', I moved on. There are people who find a calling and should stick with what they are doing, but lot's of others benefit in many ways from moving on. Pensions should not stand in the way of what might prove to be positive personal moves.

Even teachers, who we hope see their work as a calling, may find that the calling was not strong enough or their talents quite as suited to the task as they thought. Certainly our society doesn't give them the sort of respect that would encourage them when their energy flags. If they find they don't have the passion any longer, they may need to move on. Teachers require so much passion wherever they teach, but especially in areas where economic devastation adds to class size and to student problems outside the schools.

Teacher evaluations, especially those that rely on test scores, don't evaluate passion, the core ingredient of good teaching, and never will. So, let's remove any incentive teachers may have to cling to a job that no longer inspires them, incentives like pensions, and free them to move on. Maybe a good number will find

---

[64] Newark Star Ledger, 3/20/11. See article in the New Jersey section.

their way elsewhere. I may be indulging in wishful thinking here, but this more natural elimination process would do a lot less damage to education than eliminating teachers on the basis of their students' standardized testing results or on inflexible last in first out rules. Of that, I'm sure.

Fortunately for me and others who moved on, workers in the private sector accepted and in my case embraced the 401 K alternative. It's time for a 401 K for government workers. If you need to move on, you just roll that 401 K into an IRA and start over at your new job. That's your money, not money controlled by pension managers, not money somewhere out there to be picked at by vulture politicians. Is there risk? Of course there is. But you would be accepting risk as a participant in business ownership or financing. You might even take a part in financing the federal government or states and communities through bonds. There's a wealth of possibilities out there, and being more directly a part of it is way more interesting than leaving decisions to pension managers. You may make mistakes but so do pension managers. Besides, there's plenty of good advice available. And, the notion that you can't manage your own money is, frankly, insulting.

Unions need to take control of the discussion about their future, and a good place to start would be by announcing that they are ready for a transition from pensions to 401 K's. Then they will need to bargain (collectively) about just how that transition will need to proceed. They might consider a hybrid plan like TIAA-CREF provides to academics and medical researchers.[65] Whatever unions decide, they need to say, "look we are willing to move away from what we had relied on in the past, but at least for older workers (who have insufficient time to adjust) keep your word and allow them to retire based on what they were promised". There may well be other concessions unions will need to make, like concessions on medical benefits, given the condition of government finances; but, if so, it doesn't hurt politically to have made a considerable concession up front like ending pensions.

---

[65] https://www.tiaa-cref.org/public/index.html

CHAPTER 6
Healthcare

Introduction

November, 2011

I know how hard for Americans of every political persuasion what I'm about to ask will be, but I'll ask anyway. Let's consider the Affordable Health Care Act a realistic example of democracy in action, full of compromises, unloved by practically everyone; but, if recognized as a product of the democratic process we all claim to support, a basis for a workable triumph.

Compromise, well, look at what liberals gave up. There will be no single payer plan, a severe blow to the leverage that one big payer would give us to control medical costs and a blow to attempts to reduce paperwork. Liberals even gave up the government option as one of the exchange choices and with it their best chance to establish a real baseline in terms of the coverage and cost.

Conservatives, on the other hand, had to accept limits on their unrestricted free enterprise model; they had to accept some basic regulatory ground rules. There will be no cherry picking of those whom insurance companies insure within a particular exchange area. There will be no exclusions based on pre-existing conditions. They had to accept a mandate to buy insurance. And, they didn't even get to hit on mal-practice lawyers.

And what did the two sides get that they should like? Liberals got regulations preventing insurance companies from discriminating against anyone for whatever reason. They got the mandate that allows the system to afford premiums low enough to support the expansion in coverage and the allowances for those who can't afford insurance. Conservatives got an insurance market place that is free to innovate. Hopefully those insurance companies who invented the donut hole will come up with something that actually improves the system like replacing fee for service with results based care.

Here's the hard part. What we got is just what a representative democracy is likely to produce. We needed to admit that our current system was failing us in terms of costs, results and fairness, and we did. We have known about these failures for a long time and we have attempted to fix them for a long time. We now actually have a law on the books and an approach that represents a uniquely American compromise. Now that's a triumph deserving our support. What we need to do is implement it wisely and improve it, not destroy it.

The Public Option and the Mandate

June 21, 2009

The government health insurance option has become, as one might have guessed, the central issue as the health insurance debate heats up. The insurance industry does not want to compete with an alternative, federal insurance plan, no matter how open the market remains to private insurance. I just responded to my Republican congressman's email on the subject. Note how he prefaces the question of whether you support the public plan[66]:

"Earlier this month, the President called on Congress to send him health care reform legislation by October 2009. The president and his allies support a *public health insurance program*, calling it 'key to expanding coverage and controlling health care spending.'

But some congressional leaders oppose a *government-run health program* because it would lead to higher taxes, rationing of care and put *government bureaucrats* in control of decisions that should be made by families and doctors. Please share your views by answering the survey below." (Italics added by me.) Needless to say, he'll get more of my views than he is likely to read.

That second paragraph contains the arguments and distortions you can expect from the insurance companies. The '*public health insurance program*' of the first paragraph has magically transformed into a complete '*government-run health program*' in the second paragraph. Note that neither paragraph even mentions that the federal plan as proposed by Obama is an alternative you can choose. You could even

---

[66] Leonard Lance, my current representative, at least asks about issues. Michael Ferguson, the previous Republican representative, didn't bother to ask.

read Representative Lance's whole statement above as saying that the president supports only 'a public health insurance program', in other words, a single payer plan. He does not. My representative's statement is a setup, step one in shifting the argument to a single payer system, an easier target in the US. You can expect to hear that the government plan is a Trojan horse for single payer, another way to shift to the easier target rather than confront the actual proposal.

Decisions about a person's health are not now made, nor under any new proposal will they be made, by any one entity such as '*government bureaucrats*'. Doctors and other health providers help make your health decisions and remain private, now and under all current proposals. You make your own health decisions, and you always will. You smoke or don't, eat at McDonalds or don't, exercise or don't. By reducing health, decision making to a single entity, those awful '*government bureaucrats*', my representative resorts to the kind of code wording that poisons serious political discourse. We are all supposed to be horrified at the notion that '*government bureaucrats*' might interfere with our lives.

If you choose the government-run option, decisions about what to cover shift from employees of private insurers with a direct, profit based interest in denying claims to government employees with a rule based (yes, perhaps nitpicking, annoying, and bureaucratic) interest in denying claims that bend the rules or that actually might be fraudulent. *Rationing of care*? What is the denial of a claim if it isn't a form of rationed care? It's an integral part of the current system and may be among the tough decisions required for any future system. Those of us on Medicare should expect some rationing of care. For instance, do we really want to treat a 65-year-old male with prostate cancer, or even test for it, when the disease takes 30 or 40 years (I think that's right) to reach a critical stage? That decision is easy for me. Other decisions may actually require sacrifice on our part.

Higher taxes? Well, I would expect any revision that seeks to provide wider access to coverage (dare I say universal coverage) to cost more, at least initially, whether the provider is private or public or whether the cost increase takes the form of higher premiums or higher taxes[67] or both. To provide wider access, we need to be sure that private insurance companies, practicing within a particular geographic area, insure all those who request insurance in that area, regardless of age or pre-existing condition. The public plan should be equally open. That requirement means insurance companies cannot cherry-pick the healthy and therefore lower their premiums based on the resulting lower predictions of what their payouts will be, as some do now. If we believe insurance providers shouldn't be able to simply refuse to insure the sick, or to price them out of their plans, then we should expect an upward pressure on the price of premiums or taxes.

Providing a counter-balancing downward pressure on premiums or taxes, given open access, could hinge in part on a second requirement that many people find as onerous as the government insurance option. Young and healthy people should have to buy insurance too, simply put, in order to balance the higher payouts likely for the old and sick. That's why there are those who insist on a mandate forcing all to choose at least one of the health insurance options available. There may be other ways to spread the risks and therefore reduce premium costs; but none, that I know of, would have the same power as spreading the risk over the widest possible range of healthy citizens. Of course mandates would require aid for those who simply can't afford any option, and subsidizing their premiums will cost money too, maybe more, maybe less than we now pay for their way less than ideal emergency room care.

---

[67] We need to prepare ourselves to accept higher taxes; after all we've already accepted higher insurance premiums. The government has been avoiding taxes by borrowing since Reagan at an unsustainable rate. Someday we'll have to pay for what we've run up. Health care (as it is or improved) cannot be sustained forever by borrowing or printing money. As I've argued elsewhere, today is not the day; but, within the next 5 to 10 years, we will need to get serious.

If you look to private insurers or health providers to cut costs on their own, consider the fine example Paul Krugman unearthed in his June 6 op-ed piece. Apparently the former New York Times op-ed contributor, William Kristol (a neo-conservative who made me cringe) in a 1993 memo advised Republican members of congress to resist any sort of health care reform. He did, however, admit that some tinkering was needed, like a universal insurance claim form to streamline insurance paperwork.

As Krugman points out, in the 16 years since universal health insurance went down in defeat in '93, the insurance companies, left to their own devices, have not made that simple paperwork change. Health Providers could have (but haven't) created a sensible computerized record keeping system. Why should insurance companies or health providers bother with such cost saving improvements, if no one applies financial pressure? A competitive federal alternative insurance plan should act as the kick in the butt they both need. That's at least one good reason for having it.

While private plan premiums are too high, private plans do appear, at least, to reduce payments to medical providers by standardizing the cost of medical procedures. HMO's and several variants with difficult to grasp initials (PPO, PP this, and PP that) create groups of providers who agree to a procedural cost structure based on geographical area 'standard' pricing and imposed by the insurance companies. You see the difference on medical insurance payment listings as charged amounts (what the provider charged) versus accepted amounts (what the insurance company accepted). Depending on your deductible, co-payment, or whether you've fallen into a donut hole or not, you or the insurance company or both pay the lower accepted amounts.

The difference between charged amount and accepted amount can be considerable. I sometimes wonder if the charged amount is so high because providers must make up for the lower, insured figure, by charging the uninsured such high amounts. I know at least one provider who refuses to join such plans because they would force him to do exactly that.

One promising cost saving proposal goes to the heart of our current health payment system, which bases so many of the charges on the use of individual procedures rather on the overall results of the health care received. The problem with emphasizing procedures is that it provides an incentive to use procedures that might not be necessary. Add the 'CYA' incentive and you may be getting a lot more procedures than you need, or at best, the decision to order a procedure may be seriously skewed toward the unnecessary and (not incidentally) expensive.

The proposed alternative is payment based on results of medical care. I haven't read much on this approach (the details might be mind boggling), but I would guess one advantage would be an emphasis on holistic care. Payments for results should encourage what already may be a trend away from an emphasis on late phase heroic intervention (TV drama medicine) toward health maintenance over time. My own belief is that this change would give us one of the best chances to improve health care and save money. Some advocates of results based pricing think that, if medical providers (including doctors) were employees earning salaries, then good patient health results might be encouraged by giving reasonable bonuses for those results.[68]

According to a June 9 article in the N. Y. Times, congress and especially the Obama administration have shown interest in deriving medical cost savings based on research at Dartmouth that documents significant regional variations in Medicare costs per individual covered. Oddly enough McAllen, Texas was the most expensive city for health care, according to the research as reported in the Times. New York leads the states, trailed only slightly but still in the $9000+ range by New Jersey, Florida, Texas, and Louisiana. The national average is $8,304. States like

---

[68] Does anyone know whether Kaiser Permanente of California retains health care providers, including doctors, as paid employees?

Minnesota, Wyoming, Oregon, and the Dakotas are in the $6000 range. Naturally enough lawmakers from the cheap states would like to take money from the expensive states either to cover the uninsured or to supplement care in the underserved regions that they represent.

Let's hope the Obama administration is looking more deeply into the reasons for the regional disparities than those who would simply shift money from one region to another. I could come up with a number of reasons why certain regions might have higher per person medical costs than others that would not justify shifting money away including coal pollutants drifting into the East from the Midwest or higher populations that tend to increase tension and disease transmission. I can also come up with reasons that might justify penalizing less healthy states like an over-reliance on barbecues in Texas and Louisiana. I'm kidding, I love my occasional barbecue, and to hell with the health consequences. Actually, it seems the doctors connected with the McAllen, Texas hospital do more high tech surgery and testing with no better health results than less costly areas, according to the research.

If you really want cheap and effective health care, move to Canada. Nicholas Kristof's June 11 op-ed piece chronicles the story of a woman forced by job changes to do just that. She was covered under the Canadian plan and then suffered a stroke. Her care was excellent from the moment she entered the hospital (food was lousy, recovery facilities were good); money wasn't discussed. Then, after recovery, she visited San Francisco and suffered what she thought might be a relapse. This time the moment she was entered into the hospital system a clerk demanded to know her method of payment. Care had to wait. And, the overall cost per patient in the US is nearly twice as much as in Canada, according to the editorial.

Canadians do seem to understand that government programs require taxes to support them, so their tax structure might well shock US citizens. I do not experience apoplexy at tax increases, as long as those increases support needed improvements; but, like everyone else, I have my own opinions about what necessary improvements might be. Universal medical insurance qualifies for me.

Maybe the US lawmakers and the Obama administration should check out what they do in Canada to keep costs down rather than researching in Wyoming. Still, though we probably can't just substitute a Canadian style single payer system and eliminate insurance companies, those companies are right to feel a good deal of pressure. No more cherry picking of healthy clients is a bad enough hit. Adding a government-run competitor; that's competition of a scale difficult to figure.[69] They already need help competing with government run Medicare, relying on government subsidies to keep their Medicare Advantage Plans afloat. And, if we're smart, we'll keep the pressure[70] on by acting as if we just might consider the ultimate specter that haunts insurance companies and medical providers, the real cost saving health care alternative, the government run single payer system.[71]

---

[69] Those opposed to a government run option are now discussing some form of non-profit cooperative. The test for such an alternative should be whether it will have enough leverage to force private insurance companies to match the benefits by providing affordable insurance that actually pays medical bills without the usual host of excuses for not paying them.

[70] 6/21/09—news today is that Sen. Baucus (D), who is attempting to construct a bipartisan bill, has already made good use of the pressure generated by just talking about a health care plan. It seems that pharmaceutical companies have chipped in to help fill the Medicare drug donut hole for low and middle income elder citizens. That's $80 billion worth of improved care, if they're serious. The senator is reported to be bargaining with other members of the health industry.

[71] Private Insurance administrative costs versus Medicare Administrative costs—Paul Krugman responding to Heritage Foundation arguments claiming the opposite: "However, the Congressional Budget Office (CBO) has found that administrative costs under the public Medicare plan are less than 2 percent of expenditures, compared with approximately 11 percent of spending by private plans under Medicare Advantage. This is a near perfect "apples to apples" comparison of administrative costs, because the public Medicare plan and Medicare Advantage plans are operating under similar rules and treating the same population.

(And even these numbers may unduly favor private plans: A recent General Accounting Office report found that in 2006 Medicare Advantage plans spent

Whatever we do, we should keep in mind that health is a different sort of commodity than others we insure in the private marketplace. Most other things we treasure and therefore tend to insure we can do without. Our cars, our houses, our boats (that hurts), we could do without. I know people who use public transit (where available), rent, and do nicely with a canoe. Health? Some people think they can do without insuring it, but few would choose the alternative to health itself.

Those who think they can do without insuring health should talk to their friends. I'll bet that every one of them or someone close to them could come up with a nearly fatal moment, avoided by chance alone, that might have cost them everything they had, if they had survived without insurance. I can come up with several near misses in my own life. If they don't survive, then someone pays whatever medical expenses there were—family, friends, all of us (through our own higher care costs). After all, the hospitals and medical providers need to be paid too.

The following is a comment provided by one of my more passionate blog readers:

The US spends more per capita on health care than any other industrialized nation, and all the others have universal health coverage. While we spend much more, our results are worse than several other countries. Finland spends less than half per capita than we spend and ranks above us in outcomes.

Why isn't the press asking why health care expenses are so much less in these other countries, yet their outcomes are better? If we spent half what we now spend per capita, universal coverage should cost us LESS than we're paying for health care now. What huge tax increases? Why would we need them?

83.3 percent of their revenue on medical expenses, with 10.1 percent going to non-medical expenses and 6.6 percent to profits—a 16.7 percent administrative share.)"

Why aren't the Democrats pointing this out? The populace doesn't know these facts because the press doesn't cover them as it should.

Universal coverage paid for by taxes would make American companies more competitive. Employer-provided insurance costs money that companies in other countries don't have to pay. And numerous small businesses can't afford to provide any coverage to employees, or coverage is so skimpy as to be nearly useless. This is a manifestly and irredeemably unfair system that is a national shame.

Private insurance? There is *no* decent private insurance that is affordable by the majority of the population that is not earning six figures, or high five figures.

Even ignoring the fact that the US spends twice as much per capita as many other countries, universal coverage should not cost more than the total sum now—except for the additional expense of covering people who have no health care now.

Is our populace so lacking in moral compass that we'd rather have people without care than pay more? The answer is "yes" or we'd already have universal health care. My suggestion: shame the hell out of these people. Let them know we're on to their selfishness and lack of ethics. This probably won't change their minds, but at least they'll know that we're on to them and they disgust us. Universal coverage doesn't have to mean spending more. It just means we'll spend it on taxes rather than the present mishmash of insurance premiums, direct payments, taxes, higher costs throughout the system to pay for the uninsured and the differences between what insurance or the government pays and what the care actually costs, and the profit makers in the present system (excessive salaries, advertising).

Talk of rationing is ridiculous. Care is ALREADY rationed by ability to pay, accessibility of doctors and hospitals, and decisions of insurance companies and government agencies. So what would change? Nobody is proposing that people would not have a choice of doctors in a universal system, including a single-payer system. What is both amazing and sad is that so many people fall for these dumb-ass objections to real health-care reform.

I agree with you that *everyone* has to be included because it balances out the risk. You can't leave out the young, healthy people. Not only are they needed for risk balancing, but they also may need expensive care sooner than they think. Every day young people are seriously injured or become ill with expensive diseases like cancer or infections.

I'm worried about universal care's prospects. It would help if Democrats weren't so willing to roll over, if they were better informed, if they pointed out the facts about health care costs and outcomes in the US vis-a-vis other countries.

Healthcare Update

August 13, 2009

Last week I had the opportunity to discuss healthcare reform at length with my favorite doctor. I've known this doctor for all but two years of my life, which, as my children and grand children point out, is a long, long time. Discussions could hardly have been more open. She had informed answers based on her history as a physician to questions I had left unanswered in my last blog on this subject. Her history includes work as an employed doctor at Kaiser Permanente, as an administrator in charge of a division at a single facility, and then as an administrator in charge of the same division for all Kaiser Permanente facilities in Northern California. In charge meant that suggestions and complaints from hundreds of other doctors within the system were ultimately her responsibility to help implement or resolve. I can't imagine that there are many people as fully informed about how the Kaiser Permanente healthcare system works day in and day out as she is.

Fairly recently she left administration and Kaiser Permanente behind to focus on the practice of medicine again. Along with others, she began her own fee for service business, and she seems to have proven to herself and others that she can succeed at this approach to medical practice too.

So, you might ask, I hope, what does she think about the two different, private business models for delivering health care? How does the corporate model represented by Kaiser Permanente compare with the smaller, should I say mom and pop model, many of us would recognize? Her preference was clear and, for many, may be surprising. She thought that doctors had a better opportunity to be better doctors at Kaiser Permanente than as independents. Why is that, you are supposed to ask.

We can begin to develop an answer by considering what we probably already know about our own doctor's responsibilities as independents. Just walk in the office door of an independent, private practitioner and think about what you see, as I did recently. The one I visited is a well-run, local facility with two doctors and a nurse practitioner; it's nearby and happens to accept my insurance (the reason I chose it). I had to switch from one that didn't. I've grown to like the doctors, as does my wife. We haven't met the nurse practitioner yet. It's friendly, cozy, and comfortable; I couldn't ask for a more pleasant medical environment. The magazine selection is to my taste.

Adjacent to the waiting room is the usual administrative office with a simple, unimposing, wooden half door where patients like myself make themselves known to staff and present insurance information, confirm appointments, etc.. There are two, maybe three, administrators to handle these non-medical issues, pull charts, file, etc. Two nurses that I know of round out the full-time staff, and there are part time employees doing billing and referrals and a part time phlebotomist. As I wait, an extremely well dressed and attractive blond enters, makes herself known to the administrators, and takes a seat. My eyes drift from the magazine, despite all my efforts at self-discipline.

Well, the first question that occurs to me is why so many administrators and part-timers for two doctors and a nurse practitioner? It must be all those insurance forms with all those tremendously involved payment plans that occupy most of their time. Or, is it getting the insurance companies to actually pay for what they say they will pay for in their policies. My doctor's office personnel spent time recently trying to get that done for me. Add up the cost of the administrators, the nurses, the phlebotomist, and the other part-timers, and you have quite a staff for a small business to support.

We all should know by this time that the business expenses include very expensive malpractice insurance. Add rent, advertising, medical supplies, lingering student debt, profit, and whatever I've forgotten; and you no longer need to wonder why good doctors charge what they do. Oh, add in what the attractive blond was peddling to what you may end up paying too. Turns out she was a drug company rep, introducing the doctors to a new drug, perhaps. I'm hoping their heads remained clearer than mine would have when she made her case for the newest, most expensive alternative to perhaps cheaper, as effective, existing medications.[72]

Except for the drug rep reveries, many of these doctor office observations were confirmed by my Kaiser Permanente turned independent doctor friend. I'll have to ask her if the drug companies sent a Rock Hudson look alike. She, too, complained about the insurance and bill-processing overhead. She and her fellow doctor-owner employ an accountant and a general office worker. She mentioned the advertising expenses associated with a new practice and the ongoing burden of malpractice insurance. She has a family to support in an expensive area of California, so I didn't need to ask about profit, though she volunteered that the business was profitable, even though it was relatively new.

There is no doubt that these small office practices appeal to us strongly. In many of them you will see a copy of the Norman Rockwell image of a young, bare bottomed boy patient and the grandfatherly physician, the iconic picture representing all the comfortable feelings we have about this medical delivery system. But is it cost effective? My first guess is no, not really. For cost effectiveness, the Kaiser Permanente model seems likely to be

---

[72] Just so happens that I had to order an antibiotic yesterday. The out of pocket cost was $219.00 for a month's worth. Fortunately an alert pharmacist suggested a $20.00 generic. We'll double check with the doctor, who ordered the drug. Beware of drug reps peddling new drugs.

the better system. Just the sharing of facilities with many doctors rather than a couple should introduce the cost advantages of scale that item by item should run down through the system. Pooled administrators, nurses, phlebotomists, equipment, and supplies— I doubt any small operation could match the savings. And, think of the clout such an organization has when dealing with malpractice insurers, health insurers, and drug companies.

But, what about the actual healthcare the two systems deliver? My doctor friend, who, as I mentioned has practiced medicine under both, says that the Kaiser Permanente system helps improve care. I can see that not worrying about the profits, not worrying about the burden of malpractice insurance, not hassling with business concerns in general might allow a doctor to concentrate more narrowly on patients. Also, a community of doctors, there, day in and day out, would seem to me to be an invaluable resource, especially if mechanisms existed for information sharing, as, in fact, they do.

Those mechanisms include Kaiser Permanente's own specified best practices for all conditions treated, and those best practices are monitored. My doctor friend tells me that though there is a monitoring procedure, she never felt that she couldn't override the specified best practice if she thought otherwise. All she had to do was defend her opinion. That's not a bad check on individual fallibility. I would guess that the Kaiser Permanente best practices might evolve, if they haven't already, toward the results based medicine most thoughtful practitioners know is where we need to head both to improve health and contain costs.

Much of the general healthcare discussion centers on whether best practices (or results based medicine) and fees for individual procedures are compatible. Though just how fee for service effects best practices no doubt varies widely from doctor to doctor, there is some reason to worry that when the fees are tied to individual services the emphasis is likely to be on the services themselves rather than on the overall health of the patient.

Whatever incentives to overuse procedures there may be in a fee for services system, they seem to me to be less likely to operate at facilities like Kaiser Permanente. Doctors are at least one step removed from the profit motive that might entice them to rely too heavily on unnecessary and expensive procedures. Since Kaiser Permanente maintains the malpractice insurance, I'd think that individual doctors would be less driven to order CYA procedures. Besides, individual doctors have Kaiser Permanente's specified best practices to cite or the approval to override those practices, if their medical practice in a particular case is questioned, even though the Kaiser Permanente best practices are medical guidelines, not legal definitions.[73]

Unfortunately I doubt that any of these arguments for the Kaiser Permanente healthcare system will convince most Americans to consider the kind of radical changes simply adopting such a system would require. We are all very comfortable with the familiar patient/doctor relationship, and we associate that relationship with the small office practitioners we know so well. Just recognizing that their system of providing health services may not provide maximum cost efficiency or encourage the best possible medical practice probably won't be enough to alter the sense that we would lose too much, if we lost that cozy little office.

I do think that there are opportunities for the small doctor-businesses to adopt some of the methods used so effectively by organizations like Kaiser Permanente, while retaining their small town charm. I see no reason why vast numbers of independents couldn't band together into cooperatives that would match the leverage when purchasing malpractice insurance or when dealing with recalcitrant medical insurance firms. We have seen, already, medical office complexes that house many different doctors in

---

[73] There was an excellent segment on PBS (Jim Lehrer) about the Billings Montana facility that has employed doctors and runs like Kaiser Permanente. Many of the points made here about cost and care were made during this segment, and Kaiser Permanente was mentioned as a similar facility.

suites. Why wouldn't these doctors share some of the personnel and the purchasing advantages of scale as Kaiser Permanente does? There is no reason why doctors, even if dispersed, shouldn't be able to share information about best practices effectively in a networked age and why they couldn't build their own organizations to promote and even monitor the use of their own set of best practices. I would hope that most already do share information and follow some stated best practices, perhaps as formally as Kaiser Permanente does or perhaps somewhat informally at conferences, through their own organizations, or through[74] loosely structured networks of colleagues.

There are so many good ideas out there for improving healthcare and controlling costs that it is really a shame that we will be spending the months of August and September yelling simple-minded one-liners at each other and our congressmen. Before the Republican attack crowd started poisoning any real debate by shouting absurdities at public meetings, I participated in a civil exchange held as a phone conference by my Republican representative, Leonard Lance. He answered a number of questions including one of my own and helped clarify his stance, quite opposed to mine, but at least calmly and sensibly discussed. One caller caught us both by surprise when he suggested that those choosing to provide their loved ones with a living will might deserve an insurance premium break, given the disproportionate amount we spend on healthcare in the last few months of our lives. Rep-

---

[74] An NY Times op-ed (081309) by Atul Gawande, Donald Berwick, Elliot Fisher and Mark McClellan discusses cost efficiency and levels of medical care as measured nationwide based on Medicare documentation. The top performers in terms of cost efficiency that provided good care included independents and large providers like Kaiser Permanente. Apparently the independents can do the job right.

The editorial mentioned provisions in various reform bills making their way through the legislative process that have provisions "to protect successful medical communities by incorporating payment approaches that reward those that slow spending growth while improving patient outcomes." Please comment if you know anything about these measures.

resentative Lance honestly admitted that he had not heard that idea before, (I hadn't either) and that he would think about it.[75] He'll have to talk it over with those crafting the 'grandpa killing' lines currently endorsed by the rabid Republican playbook and spouted by the likes of Sarah Palin.

I've often wondered what would happen if someone like Sarah Palin actually sat down privately and discussed an idea. Maybe they could discuss an idea I heard presented on ABC one morning recently. There are doctors out there who have devised a 'flat fee' payment system. The idea is to pay a monthly fee ($79 was the amount mentioned) that would cover all of a primary physician's expenses for your care during the year, no matter what that care might involve in the way of the doctor's time and expense.

The doctor would limit the number of patients he would take on (800 was mentioned by one of the two interviewed) so that the time per patient would remain reasonable. Insurance companies and the doctor office expense of dealing with them would disappear for these providers. There would be no need to insure in order to cover what you have already paid for up front. Insurance companies would have to be content with insuring against emergencies that would involve medical treatment beyond the primary physician's scope.

Sarah Palin could respond that she thought that might encourage the doctor to cut corners on care, since the money

---

[75] Apparently neither of us caught a provision in at least one of the bills providing Medicare money for discussing living wills with your doctor. Even discussing it is apparently a Nazi like, death squad proposal to some of the shouters out there. Imagine what they would say if we actually encouraged such sensible behavior with a premium reduction.

Shame on you, Sarah Palin. You've managed to so distort the issue that you end up equating our local doctors with a death panel. It really is difficult to talk with someone who confuses a doctor/patient discussion with what she called 'Obama's death panel.' I'll just say it—anyone who does not consider specifying the medical measures to be taken at the end of life is not thinking about those left behind who will need to talk to the doctor about those measures. Those decisions are very hard to make and enforce without specific direction from the patient.

comes in even if he/she does nothing. A defender of the flat fee could respond that perhaps the doctor might take a more holistic approach to medicine and cut down on unnecessary procedures, since there would be no profit motive for ordering them. They could both consider looking at how the system works in practice. If we are going to solve the immense problems of healthcare coverage, quality, and cost inherent in our current system we are going to have to do our research, sit down, and talk. Time to get started; so, let's just ignore the media's emphasis on battle lines and get on with the thinking we need to do.

Note:

The December 7, 2009 edition of Newsweek has an article on the Cleveland Clinic. It makes the same points about the efficiency of large medical organizations and salaried doctors as I do in this blog entry, except for one. The only mistake I seem to have made is that the problem of dealing with health insurance companies is as bad for the Cleveland Clinic as it is for the mom and pop organizations. The article states that it takes 1400 clerks to handle the insurance claims for 2000 doctors. Blows my mind.

Responses to Healthcare Blog Entries

August 27, 2009

I got a number of responses to my last two entries on healthcare from regular readers with varied political allegiances. I'm gratified to note that my liberal, conservative, and libertarian friends, and even those like myself with a mishmash of political instincts can exchange views while remaining civil.

That said, I'd add that several responses did not lack in passionate intensity. A couple of readers and I are in heartfelt agreement that there are limits to extending civility, and those limits have been exceeded by the 'death panel' crowd and by those like the woman who confronted Barney Frank with the portrait of Obama festooned with a Hitler style mustache. As one friend pointed out, there is no reason to extend civility to them, and Barney Frank was quite right to ignore the woman's opinions as unworthy of any consideration. The difference between my friends' responses and the over-televised town meeting exchanges is that my friends included reasoned arguments backed by references to what is and is not in the various bills and by facts about our healthcare system (if what we have can be called a system) and other systems.

One friend got at an issue avoided altogether or stepped around gingerly by our politicians. Why, he asked, do we allow the words profit and healthcare to occur in the same conversation? There is just something uncomfortable about profiting from peoples' illnesses. No other economically advanced nation allows profit to intrude so casually into the field of healthcare.[76] For the US, especially among the neo-cons, profit seems to have reached sacred status, and when we make something sacred, by definition we put it beyond rational discussion. It's time to de-sanctify it and discuss it, especially if we intend to hand over millions of new, healthy customers to insurance companies by mandating health insurance for all. That's a potential profit bonanza that we just can't allow without giving it some thought. Here's a stock tip. If it looks like the public insurance option is going down to defeat, buy into health insurance companies and make a killing. Too late, better stock pickers have already raised the prices.

We worship profit in part because we believe it spurs innovation, and we have plenty of evidence that in fact it does. But, we ought to look at just what sort of innovation we are getting out of the profit motive in various areas of healthcare. Health insurance innovation has brought us deductibles, co-pays, donut holes (my favorite), yearly maximums, life-time maximums, provider networks (or can't see your own doctor networks), and legal documents in the guise of benefit policy statements that should be and could be readable but aren't. Most would look at the I-phone and cheer on innovation and profit, but one look at that health insurance list would be more likely to illicit a Bronx cheer.

---

[76] Several European countries with universal healthcare like the Netherlands and Switzerland allow insurance company profit, or did. But, the government regulates the industry strictly including a cap on allowable profits. See http://www.commonwealthfund.org for a PDF on health insurance in these two countries. Somewhere I heard that the profit taking is no longer allowed. The article may be behind the times. Note that both have a public option and both have active private insurance plans. Both mandate insurance for all citizens. None of the European systems I am aware of simply assumes that profit is naturally self regulating because of competition as we do. The author (T. R. Reid, The Healing of America) pointed out that there is still robust competition among health insurance companies in Switzerland based on the number of insured, because the more members that a company insures the better the pay for executives. That's enough incentive without adding profit. He mentions that Switzerland changed the for profit model to a non-profit model recently after the 'for profit' companies started refusing coverage based on pre-existing conditions. The Swiss wouldn't put up with such unjust treatment.

Of course there are those, I assume (I didn't hear from any), who would argue that the health insurance industry innovations have controlled the cost of care explosion. Somehow that argument seems to me weak on the face of it given the explosion we've had anyway. But, whatever you think might have happened to costs without insurance company innovation, there are better ways to control such costs. I've already described the Kaiser Permanente (KP) model and its possible cost control advantages.[77]

Part of the cost issue can be quite simply stated. What do medical personnel want from their careers? In most economically advanced countries, the answer would seem to be good pay and the chance to practice their craft. I would bet that the majority of those practicing medicine in the US would find such a life sufficiently rewarding. I'd also bet that cluttering up that life with business related concerns and with insane amounts of health-insurance company paperwork would not add all that much to their overall experience.

Consider the French doctor interviewed by T. R Reid.[78] When a patient came in, the doctor simply ran their medical card and viewed all necessary medical information. Then the same card billed the insurance company with the click of a key. There were no arguments about coverage. Sounds like that doctor might have had time for his patients and a leisurely French lunch perhaps with a glass of red wine. Why wouldn't medical providers like that?

---

[77] Technically KP has three divisions—health plan, doctor groups, and hospitals. Theoretically the health plan and hospitals are not for profit, the doctor groups, for profit, though there is considerable skepticism about the meaning of these terms when applied to the vast amounts of money floating around in the KP divisions. Incidentally I found out how KP handles malpractice insurance. KP simply covers any costs themselves. Suits are brought against KP, not individual doctors. And, they defend KP vigorously, as you can well imagine. A couple of readers brought up tort reform and malpractice insurance as concerns. I'm not informed enough to write anything about either, but I do think that having individual doctors attempting to cover themselves is just one more expense and hassle they don't need.

[78] I'm relying on interviews. The book, see above, sounds like it's worth a read.

If there is a place for profit in the health field, I'd think the clearest case could be made for the pharmaceutical industry. Creating, testing, and gaining approval for drugs is a very long-term proposition with lots of costly but unproductive attempts along the way.[79] High risk, long-term investment of capital—that sounds like what profit is meant to encourage. When I first heard that the pharmaceutical industry had offered $80 billion to cover the Medicare drug donut hole over the next 10 years, I thought; well, good, somebody's willing to pitch in. Then I heard just what a measly amount that was compared to projected profits. And, I began to think about what they might want in return. Did they buy a no shopping around for generic or foreign alternatives clause somewhere? It would help if I knew the details. None-the-less I can see the need for profit here; I guess all I would argue is how much.

There's one part of the healthcare equation we have left out by discussing profit, and that's the patients. It seems to me that at the core of our discussion of the cost problem we need to include what we all want out of health care. First we need to take the same moral stand other economically advanced nations have taken (including Thailand incidentally). We need to insist that basic medical care is a right not the privilege we make of it currently. I do not understand how a nation that claims to be largely Christian could possibly continue to maintain otherwise. Something of Jesus' response to others (including the least favored) ought to rub off on Christians. You'd think other religions would feel the same compulsion. Healthcare is a basic civil right, and we need to view it that way, as Jonathan Alter pointed out in a recent 'Newsweek' opinion piece. Appealing to the 'what's in it for me' crowd might be a necessary political strategy that our president needs to follow, but I would hope that in this case he's wrong to think so. I'd prefer he make healthcare reform a call to our better instincts.

Recognizing healthcare as a right does not have to mean that we are somehow absolving certain members of our society from

---

[79] 89% of drugs that reach the human clinical trial stage are cancelled. That's risk for you. Of course that doesn't even count all the work done on drugs that never reach the human stage of testing.

responsibility for their own health costs. We need to start hammering away at what we can all do today and every day. Take our addiction to soda. One can of soda provides nearly 3 times the daily-recommended intake of sugar. Add in the corn syrup and other sweeteners in cereals and any number of other packaged foods, stir in a sedentary life style, and America's overwhelming problem with obesity isn't hard to understand.

Cut out the soda, have a good, old shot of American Bourbon instead. Sweeten your cereal yourself with fruit or honey; try some spices on food. Avoid elevators, use stairs, walk. If we don't attack obesity, we'll simply continue to spend nearly 1 out of 5 dollars of our Medicare outlay on diabetes alone.[80] We'll continue as the heart attack, coronary disease chumps of the world. We just can't afford this kind of self-neglect anymore. Do I want a tax on sodas? Why not? We don't seem able to do what we need to do to extend our own lives; maybe putting wallets in danger would work.[81] Or, maybe we could take a baby step by stopping the subsidies we hand out for corn used as corn syrup.

And, while I'm losing my cool flailing out at people, I might as well take a swing at grandma and grandpa too. Note—I'm in this group and on Medicare. I have as much trouble confronting the basic facts of my situation as anyone else of 'advanced years'. But face those facts we must. We now know we're closer to the end of life than we believed we were in our youth. We'll begin to feel a few

---

[80] Mathematica Policy Research Inc. study.

[81] I'm aware that certain Liberals consider taxes of this sort regressive. But, I'd ask them if we couldn't come up with a trade-off here. We could say that healthcare is a right not a privilege, and then chip in for those who can't afford healthcare, as we should. But, we could ask something of those receiving help too. Eat smarter or pay a tax. We might also advertise just how out of all reason American food portions tend to be. Last night 5 of us sat down to eat 4 portions of macaroni with tuna, onion, olives, and celery. We followed the portion instructions on the box. Three of the portions ended up as leftovers, and we were all filled up. In a recent sub ad, two NY ballplayers attempt to top each other's descriptions of big, referring to the subs they are eating. Each sub looks like it would feed six. They'll need steroids to digest those things. Where's the counter to these absurd standards?

aches and pains we didn't feel before. I've noticed a couple, myself. But, we might want to look at the perks too. No one is suggesting that we hobble off to Iraq or Afghanistan to serve our country and really risk life and limb immediately; that's for the young. That's for those we will be asking to pay for our Medicare, eventually. Many of us will die before the bill comes due, though the number of us likely to experience that 'happy' outcome is dwindling as the date of the financial collapse of Medicare approaches closer and closer and as we refuse to deal with that fact more and more adamantly.

Instead of yelling inanely 'don't let government mess with my Medicare' couldn't we oldsters contribute something to the health-care solution? T. R Reid (see notes), in several recent interviews described his travels around the world investigating various medical solutions offered for his less than flexible shoulder. The US was all gung ho to go in there, operate, and replace the offending body part. Read tens of thousands of dollars and a slight life risk, as with any surgery. The British told him to go home; stiff upper lip, you know. Life is not all that bad just because you can't move your shoulder like you used to. The French said they could operate, but why? In India he got massage therapy with oils; that helped, felt good, and didn't cost thousands; he didn't die and the results lasted. Some cultural adjustment might be in order for us oldsters as we fret over our aches and pains. And, if we haven't made clear in writing how we want to be treated at the end of our life, we should do that now. How silly not to.

Note:

I took the following from a Consumer Report article (March, 2008):

Lawyers: Malpractice-insurance premiums and liability awards account for less than 2 percent of overall health-care spending, according to a 2004 study by the Congressional Budget Office. Defensive medicine, the practice of ordering extra tests or procedures to protect against lawsuits, might add another few percentage points, according to some estimates. Yet 60 percent of respondents blamed lawyers for high costs, and 69 percent specifically pointed to "frivolous lawsuits."

Health-care consumers: "Modifiable" risk factors, such as eating too much, exercising too little, or smoking, are to blame for an estimated 25 percent of U.S. health-care costs, according to expert estimates. But even if every American took up healthful living overnight, our health-care expenses would still be the second highest in the world (after Luxembourg). Sixty-eight percent of respondents thought those bad habits were to blame for high U.S. health costs. A mere 41 percent of respondents blamed consumers for overusing services.

Respondents to the survey could choose more than one option. That's why numbers add up to more than 100%. I'm just picking out a couple of options. The article is worth a read to gain perspective on costs vs. attitudes towards those costs. http://www.consumerreports.org/health/doctors-hospitals/health-care-security/who-is-to-blame-for-high-costs/health-care-security-costs.htm

Note that malpractice costs have been on a downward trend. More recent estimates are as low 1.5%.

Angry Letter to my Representative, After Healthcare Vote

August 27, 2009

Representative Lance,

I am disappointed in your vote on this historic attempt to align the US health care system with other countries that have the means to extend this critical life line to all citizens. More than anything else, I consider failure to cover our fellow citizens a moral failure, and I'm constantly surprised to see a party that claims support from a group calling itself the 'moral majority' consistently proving that they don't take the biblical injunction about the least of these seriously. I am disappointed in you personally because I have admired the energetic way you have elicited comment from your constituents. I had hoped you were capable of breaking from the party line when the stakes were so high.

I consider the Republican alternative at best cover (so they can say we support reform too) at worst a sham. It does not address coverage, 2 to 3 million more covered should embarrass you. You do not address the central concern of those who are required to seek insurance on their own—pre-existing conditions. I assume you do not do so because you do not support the mandate for all citizens to purchase insurance. The two go together; as I am sure you are aware.

I do not pretend to be familiar enough with the law to advise you on tort reform, one of the other Republican hobby-horses. It does seem like a weak attempt to muddy the waters; it is worth somewhere between 1 and 5 % of medical costs, depending on how you do the figuring. The high end assumes a lot of unnecessary procedures of the CYA variety; just how many actually occur would seem to me to be difficult to determine.

Also, you know, often enough, there are cases where patients deserve to be compensated. It's delicate business to determine those cases that deserve compensation and those that don't. That's why we have courts and, yes, lawyers. But, I'm sure you know this too. I'd be surprised to find that the Republican prattle about tort reform is fooling a large segment of the public by plugging some nebulous resolution of this issue as a major contribution to health care reform.

The only Republican position that may have merit seems to me to be allowing purchase of policies across state lines. I'd support that if the measure included an answer to the major objection. There are states that allow insurance companies to offer policies that are at best lacking in critical benefits at worst deceptive. Any such measure should include some regulation from the federal government, so that there is not a rush to the lowest denominator. You might consider the Medicare Supplement model that specifies coverage for various plans, Plans A through K, the last I checked. I know, Republicans don't like federal involvement, but maybe occasionally they could think out of their boxes.

One more point. We are dealing with an extremely complex problem. Some say health care is 1/6th of our economy. Why wouldn't such an extensive revision, dealing with decades of encrusted anomalies, take 1900 hundred pages to lay out a real plan that brings us closer to sanity? Every time I see a Republican smart alack slam down the bill on his desk as if we can all see from its size just how absurd it is, I think how feeble minded that representative must be.

I'm somewhat sorry for the tone of this, but I am really passionate about this issue. Your staff treated me well when I presented them with three blog entries on the issue recently. And I thank them and you for their considerate behavior.

Rich Miner (7th District, and unlikely to move)

Republican Healthcare Plan

February 1, 2010

Last week I listened in on one of my congressman's constituent call-in sessions. I was struck by just how unchallenging the questions were—softballs like 'isn't all that corruption in Washington just horrible'. Well, yes it is; except for a few cynics like me, most agree that it's just horrible. Not as horrible as the mafia that practically governs Naples or an Afghan government running as if corruption is just another expense of doing business at all levels, but horrible none-the-less. I still think there are honest, hard working congressmen in Washington, and I have yet to run across a situation where I considered the possibility that bribing a local government official or law officer might help me out. But, though I don't like Washington corruption, I fail to see where one can go in responding to such a statement. The congressman agreed that corruption is bad, too. Other questions or laments from my fellow citizens seemed as directionless as complaining about corruption in Washington.

My congressman, unlike the callers, seemed to have his act together. His primary pitch features the familiar, scary, budget deficit with the usual corollary that the bloated Democratic Healthcare bill will make it all so much worse. I believe he is sincerely worried about the deficit, and it worries me too. That's why I listened carefully for any suggestions he might have had to deal with it, especially any healthcare solutions, since healthcare is such a large part of looming deficits. And, yes, he had suggestions that he named in the process of extolling the alternative Republican healthcare bill now languishing in committee. He referred to two major provisions of the bill—tort reform and purchase of insurance policies across state lines. During the time I listened, (I finally got bored with soft-balls and responded to my wife's suggestion that I help with I forget what) he did not fill in one detail about either. I wanted to call him on the lack of detail, but the questions generating in my mind never congealed into anything I could condense sufficiently, and besides I hadn't read the bill, so how could I ask a directed question? Essentially I didn't have my act together.

Since then I've spent time reading the Republican healthcare bill HR 3970. Search on—H.R. 3970: Medical Rights and Reform Act of 2009, if you'd like to join in the fun. I've come to some conclusions on tort reform, not on the across state lines proposal.[82] Tort reform comes up in Title II, Subtitle B, Section 211 under the title of 'Help Efficient, Accessible, Low-cost, Timely Healthcare.' That's a lot for tort reform to accomplish or even help.

Most estimates put the burden of tort law at 2% to 5% of overall medical costs. Those figures include the premium costs of malpractice insurance, settlement costs, and an estimate of how much in the way of extra, unnecessary procedures may be performed simply to avoid the possibility of a malpractice law-suit. The premium cost and settlement figures might well be solid enough but the estimate on extra procedures can't be all that easy to determine. When a doctor orders a scan, how can you possibly determine if he or she ordered it fearing a lawsuit or fearing a tumor? Never mind, though I wonder about the figures, I've not heard them vigorously attacked. If the figures are right, then, judging from how often Republicans mention tort reform, they must believe that attacking 2% to 5% of healthcare costs with vigorous tort reform has the potential to significantly control medical costs.

---

[82] At this point I don't see much difference between the health exchanges in the health bill that passed and opening up nationally all the state options, as described in the Republican bill, except that control becomes state centered rather than national. I'll have to compare the two bills more carefully. Also, I should note that other portions of the bill, like sections on pre-existing conditions and medical record- keeping, sound promising as likely areas of compromise.

When I first managed to find the section on tort reform under its well-disguised title (see above), I must admit to imagining that a Republican solution would somehow attempt to cap compensatory damages directly, supporting medical institutions against patients. It helps sometimes to confront one's prejudices with a few facts—the section starts by acknowledging the legitimate compensatory needs of patients injured through malpractice. There is even an acknowledgement that punitive damages have a place in litigation, though the cap suggested seems likely to be little more than a slap on the wrist to the offending parties.

So, it would seem that the restrictions on tort law, touted as a major answer to our medical expense issues, are much more subtle than my imaginings. If I'd just thought about it a bit more, I probably could have guessed the solution. It's designed to save money at the expense of the lawyers bringing the suits against the providers. Ambulance chasers certainly make fine villains; even I tend to cringe when I see their TV ads. Caps get quite specific when it comes to their compensation or cut of the action. It seems that the purpose of the Republican tort reform is to make it less attractive for lawyers to litigate. Lawyers on the side of patients just won't get paid as well, and—to the good—patients will get more of the settlement money, if there is any.

Apparently, in this case, the free market is not capable of setting appropriate prices for services rendered. And, I guess I wonder if medical establishments will voluntarily show equal restraint, uncontrolled by government, in terms of the amounts they pour into their counter defenses. That seeming inequality aside, I think I approve of the Republican government imposed limits on free enterprise in this case. Sick people shouldn't be ripped off by lawyers, just as they shouldn't be preyed on by insurance companies.

With compensation for injuries and punitive damages still in place, though modified, and with lawyers still able to make money, though limited, one wonders just how effective tort reform will be in reducing the costs represented by the targeted 2% to 5% of medical expenses. If you dig just a bit more into the details, you'll find a connection between punitive damages and compensatory payments. Punitive damages are set at $250,000, or at no more than twice the amount of compensatory damages, whichever is higher. Though I need to know current law to be sure, the connection would seem to give medical providers a bit of added incentive to spend even more money on their lawyers to keep compensatory awards as low as possible. On the face of it, that seems like another jab at the sick, but perhaps it would help reduce the overall expense.

Such calculations of effect on purely economic grounds seem to me to hide more compelling reasons why medical personnel and medical institutions would wish to avoid malpractice suits. They all have carefully fostered reputations, reputations that even in economic terms might well encourage the overuse of expensive but unnecessary procedures to protect. It is the overuse of procedures that causes the major portion of the expense and it is the attempt to estimate that expense that is the wild card in the calculations too. Tort reform seems to me like a fairly indirect, somewhat unfair, and quite possibly ineffective way to address decisions about the use of particular procedures in individual cases. As I've harped on in previous blog entries, institutions that have addressed this issue directly, like Kaiser Permanente, provide their personnel with guidelines for the use of procedures along with processes for overriding those guidelines when individual circumstances or the individual judgments of a practitioner suggest otherwise.

If we really want to control the costs, we could begin by finding ways to encourage those who address the issue directly. Government might help. An appropriate agency could distribute research funds to back efforts, already well underway, which seek to establish reasonable guidelines for treatment. I see no need for enforcement of any results that might emerge from research; results will work their way through medical journals and networks until they build enough confidence at the level of the individual physicians and patients to change practice.

The only danger is that insurance companies will jump on research results too early, leading the change rather than following it. Government would need to see to it that insurance companies do not misuse the results in this way. Of course we'd all need to overcome the tea-party attempts to brand any progress in this direction as government coming between patient and doctor. But, perhaps, we can work our way past such attempts to brand research and science as government meddling.

Speaking of branding, the death panel harangue seemed for a while to have poisoned sensible discussion of any end of life provisions. Too bad for any real attempts to restrain medical spending; after all, a large portion of useless and really expensive medical procedures tend to occur in one's last days. Suggesting that an insurance premium break might be extended to people who were sensible and caring enough to provide living wills directing their family and medical personnel during the last days met with a wall of misinformed anger.

Without a living will, medical personnel are left with the "all possible means to extend life option", often the worst option. Family may well end up with a burden of guilt they don't need, no matter what is decided. Even the mild version, adding an insurance provision to pay for doctor/patient consultations on the subject prior to illness, brought out the full, uninformed fury of the Sarah Palin mentality. I have been somewhat encouraged to see this thoughtless distortion fading from public discussion.

But, if you really want to run into a political wall, try actually addressing the real medical cost explosion, try suggesting anything that might save us from the soon to occur disappearance of the Medicare reserves. Discussions about unnecessary procedures and end of life issues become particularly heated when the context becomes Medicare as opposed to overall healthcare. There can be no serious discussion of future deficits without addressing this problem, and almost everyone who reads a newspaper knows it. And yet, Politicians on the left, center, and right all run. Citizens aren't much better, and even our president passed control of the real deficit generators like Medicare on to a commission for study. Congress couldn't even manage that much political courage.

So, after beginning to get my act together, I ask my congress-man the following questions:

How would you handle the overwhelming deficits that will come soon when programs like Medicare go broke?

Would you be in favor of increased Medicare paycheck deduc-tions?

Would you consider reductions in coverage and if so what reductions?

Would you be in favor of at least supporting a special commis-sion to look into ways to save Medicare and reduce the real deficit threat?

Would you be willing to empower the commission with the authority to draft solutions that would then require congress to pass a bill incorporating those solutions on an up or down vote?

Would you support increased funds for research into medical procedure guidelines?

Would you consider an insurance premium reduction for those willing to invest in a living will?

Would you support an insurance option or requirement to provide for discussions between doctors and patients about liv-ing wills?

If the answers to the above questions are largely negative, why do you consider yourself serious about deficit reduction?

I'll email him or mail him a copy of this blog entry. I still haven't figured out how to boil this all down into something appropriate for a phone conference question.

CHAPTER 7
Education

Introduction

November, 2011

I only wrote one blog entry on education, but I think about education and read about it as often as I do subjects covered in other chapters. I even have a modicum of experience in the field having spent several years teaching college students. I hasten to add, though, that I know nothing about inner-city schools or any schools below college level, just conjecture based on what I hear and read.

Perhaps the lack of real experience has led me to become even more radical in terms of educational solutions than I am on other subjects, though my lack of real experience extends well beyond education. Maybe I'm more passionately radical about education because I experienced the results of our educational system. Too many college freshman with a few notable exceptions seemed to get stuck after step one or two in any attempt to argue on almost any issue.

Put quite simply, I do not believe any testing ever improved the ability to reason, the one result of successful education I consider crucial. I believe better teachers improve thinking and therefore education. The single entry in this chapter pleads my case.

Childhood Left Behind

November 15, 2009

But that little boy painted flowers
In neat rows of green and red
And when the teacher asked him why
This is what he said. and he said

Flowers are red, green leaves are green
There's no need to see flowers any other way
Than the way they always have been seen.

Writer: CHAPIN, HARRY F.
Copyright: Lyrics © Warner/Chappell Music, Inc. (Alfred Music Publishing)

I can't help thinking that the teaching forced on teachers by 'No Child Left Behind' testing has the potential of leaving behind what it is to be a child, saddling society with children like the one who has been defeated by the end of Harry Chapin's song rather than encouraging the creative children we need. That there are single right ways to see things or right answers to questions worth asking, answers that can be graded right or wrong, seems to me both an adult notion and, in significant ways, either a boring or, in many cases, an outright wrong notion.

Let's take the simplest example I can imagine in that field of all fields, mathematics, where the right answer is most often thought to be the right answer, no further questions asked. If my grand-daughter, influenced as she might be by her silly gramps, answered the question what does '1 + 1' equal with '10', then she would have to be graded wrong on most standard tests, I would guess. But, of course, I would argue that she would be closer to correct and much more thoughtful than most students would be answering '2'. She's more correct because more counting occurs in binary than in decimal, despite the fact that we have '10/ten' fingers, and more thoughtful because she thought to answer based on something she heard once or twice or maybe three times from gramps rather than simply repeating what she learned in school today and yesterday and the day before and, and...

If there is anything children do well, naturally, it's asking questions. "Why is the sky blue", anyway? I still don't really understand the answer, but it's a good question. Why would we not encourage a child's natural interest in knowing, not by answering them but by exploring the possible answers with them? After all, the important questions simply don't have easy answers; they require a process that includes gathering information, evaluating evidence, perhaps experimenting, perhaps even creativity, nothing that's easy to test by checking boxes A, B, C or D. It's opening them up to the processes of thought that ought to be the core purpose of teaching, not just answers.

When I think back many, many years to the facts I learned in High school, all I can remember is the part of the Latin conjugation of hic-hoc that starts with horum. I wonder why. What I do remember and use almost every day is certainly not a fact I memorized; it's the incredible power of Latin and other language derivations to enhance my understanding of English. And, that it's worth my time to go to the dictionary much more often than I would have if Mr. Lynch, my Latin teacher, had not in some hard to describe way made learning a dead language engaging. Others in the class remember being engaged by the ruler he carried or the cord to the blinds he handled in a somewhat menacing manner, but I like to think what engaged me even more was his passion for a language no one else cared a fig about.

Real education happens when students are passionately engaged in asking questions and teachers and students are passionately engaged in exploring answers together. Without the passion, classrooms become a gigantic bore. With it, even rote memory can come alive, as it did for me in Mr. Lynch's class. I'm going to just out and out declare that anything interfering with a passion for questioning and exploring is not going to lead America toward better education. If testing reduces education to a boring and passionless experience then testing has to go.

Of course, it might be possible to test or at least evaluate the education offered without destroying it.[83] But, if what I heard from one disgruntled 5th grade teacher recently is as general as I fear it might be, chances are slim that the testing associated with 'No Child Left Behind' is anything but damaging. Prior to the implementation of 'No Child Left Behind' directed teaching, she had created class projects that involved her students in lively historical recreations; after, there was no time. Think of that—no time to be creative.

If we really want to improve education, rather than simply generating feel good statistics based on irrelevant tests and perhaps

---

[83] The correct way to evaluate teachers ought to begin with some definition of good teaching. Bill and Melinda Gates have just made a large grant available to selected schools that seem to be doing something right. A portion of the money (a $45 million dollar portion) will go toward answering this question. This project 'will use cameras, student surveys and other tools to identify the characteristics of outstanding teachers' according to a New York Times article (Nov. 20, 2009). I'd be interested in knowing what the other tools might be. Also, I look forward to the results.

manipulated test scores[84], then we need to make a start by thinking about those who choose to teach. First, we need to encourage their interest in the subjects they teach. I'm convinced that teachers cannot engage students without being engaged themselves. Teachers can't just absorb a body of knowledge and then teach from that knowledge for the rest of their careers. They need to be model students themselves, learning more and more as they go; otherwise the students they teach miss seeing in them the passion that drives learning.

I don't think there is any limit to what can be learned about any subject, but there are limits to an individual's willingness to invest time and energy in learning. It is critical that we understand that our teachers need the time to learn, and if they then fail to invest the energy, we need to let them know that they cannot teach without making that investment.

We should follow Google's[85] lead and give teachers 20 % of their paid time to think on their own, one day a week or the equivalent. If they teach English, let them write. If they teach history, let them dig into primary documents. If they teach science, let them study the latest research or do research themselves. I would think such a program would begin as a pilot project, perhaps at charter schools, and then over time become more generally acceptable. But, if we fail to make this investment in them, we fail them and their students.

The advantages of such an investment seem obvious to me for upper grades, but I can imagine some question about whether those who teach the younger children would need the same kind of immersion in subject matter. Perhaps their subject matter might at least in part be the nature of learning at different ages.

---

[84] As I understand the testing, standards are up to the states. Perhaps I'm overly suspicious, but I can't believe that with so much riding on showing improvement that some states and school districts aren't finding ways to rig results.

[85] Google allows employees to invest 20% of their working time on their own projects. The company claims many innovations have come from this unstructured investment in their personnel.

It's a subject that has always been controversial and it's under constant investigation. Better understandings of brain development and functioning are accelerating as science finds new techniques for conducting research. Teachers need to be involved in understanding the teaching implications of new discoveries, and they need to be creatively involved in developing appropriate implementation for their classrooms.[86]

That said, I still think a real interest in subject matter translates into better teaching, at any level. Last summer I got interested in filming insects in my backyard garden. The honey bee disaster spurred me to think about the possibility that other pollinators would fill the gap. Soon my grandchildren were running around turning up rocks and searching out any little creature that moved. Interest is infectious no matter what age, and though they may not have grasped my point about pollinators (not often found underground), they were engaged and might have learned a thing or two, as I did.

Susan Engel wrote an op-ed piece in the NY Times recently (Nov. 2, 2009) making the same point about continuing, subject matter education for teachers. She went on to discuss mentoring of younger teachers, just as young doctors and nurses in the best institutions are mentored. She urged us to invest in teachers as if we respect them in the same way we respect doctors, and we should pay them as if we respect them too. We may not be able to see the immediate benefits of such an investment as we do with our investment in medical care. Bodies so obviously fail, we get sick, our loved ones and friends get sick, and we can't help but notice. But minds, it's not so obvious when they fail, we don't see

---

[86] The NY Times today had a fine article on the connection between new brain science and education. The article connected the new science with the need to develop new educational programs, exactly my point in this entry. Teachers need time to absorb the science and translate the results into better education. The article featured educators who had succeeded by creatively integrating the science into their teaching methods.

the creeping societal illness that results from lackluster education as clearly or as immediately.

Al Gore makes a similar point about short term thinking and the problems of gearing up support for real action on global warming. A global disaster with severe effects that will sneak up on us over the next 30 to 50 years just doesn't get our attention in the same way the carefully measured, current jobless rate does, even though in the scale of things global warming is a much more formidable problem. In education it's easier to watch year to year improvements in meaningless test score numbers than to consider the much more difficult to contemplate, real improvements in students' ability to cope creatively that truly engaged and supported teachers would bring 10 to 15 to 20 years down the line.

Back in October, Thomas Friedman (NY Times op-ed 10/21/2009) laid out the long term stakes. Without better education, American workers simply won't be able to compete globally. The new, high paying jobs will require innovative minds, the kind Google encourages by allowing its creative personnel time to think on their own. It's these jobs we want our children to be seeking, and we don't get them there by boring them in school. We either figure out better ways to engage them in creative thought or lose out to countries that do. It takes long term thinking on our part to develop the educational techniques and the teachers to get us there. Tests are simply politically convenient, sugar highs by comparison with what we really need.

On Observing a Windfall Oak
Grammy, why don't all the trees fall,
When the wind blows so hard?

     Ah, little one,
Strange, isn't it, this one and not that one.
They all look like the wine glass

I shattered the other day.
Just a breath of a touch
And over it went.
Much too much on top
And not much base to keep it up just right.

Could be that what we see of trees
Is not all there is to see.
Maybe, unlike the glass, way underground,
They're anchored, seized upon the earth so firm
That most trees stand up to winds.

Grammy, I can't see what's underground.
How will I ever know?
Well, I suppose we'll need a shovel.
We'll dig up a survivor,
And see what we shall see.
Perhaps, they have roots of steel
Or maybe they go all the way down to China.

Grammy, I'm serious.
Those trees are much too big,
We can't just dig one up.

No, I suppose you're right, we can't.
Not even Pop pop's backhoe would do.
Let's take on something we can handle,
Say, this dandelion, here,
With a head and leaves we see,
And perhaps, below ground,
Like the tree, much we do not see.

Grammy, look, it goes way down,
It grabs the earth and wriggles round a rock.
It branches out, and keeps on going down.
There seems no end to it.

I bet an oak's at least that smart
And hugs the earth and rocks,
Whenever hard winds begin to blow.

Writer: Gramps
Printed by permission of: Grammy

Note:

Before I finished tinkering with this blog entry, I got into a discussion at a party with another teacher. This one had left teaching music in schools for an independent career teaching yoga and martial arts. (Talk about creative.) She had complaints about 'No Child Left Behind' too, but she added that there was a real drop in curiosity somewhere between 3d grade and middle school. She'd taught both and left after enduring middle school students for a relatively short time. She mentioned that she felt the age of this loss seemed to have dropped over the years.

One has to wonder why this is happening and hope someone out there is studying the problem. If they are lost before they even reach high school, I suspect we won't see much improvement in the drop-out rate. Incidentally, if we must measure schools, then improvement in the drop-out rate would be better than wasting time and energy on testing. At least drop-out rate measures a school's ability to keep students engaged in education, and that's what's valuable.

CHAPTER 8
Bank Bailout and Stimulus

Introduction

November, 2011

If there is any area of political concern a citizen might have good reason to just plain give up on trying to understand, that area would have to be economics. It's frustratingly nerdy. I think in this case a few simple signposts help. Middle class income and the stock market stalled over the eight years of the Bush (2) administration, only the debt increased. The current recession started before Obama took office. President Bush initiated the bailout— one of his few sensible moves in my opinion. The success of the bailout required unpopular but necessary decisions, and, yes, the bailout was successful in economic terms. Politically it has cost the Obama administration dearly, even though they did not initiate it and even though their execution was successful.

Another fact needs emphasis. We went into the recession with an unnecessary fiscal handicap. President Clinton (and yes with help from Newt Ginrich) managed to balance the budget and create a surplus. President Bush followed by creating a deficit, reducing taxes on the wealthy while failing to consider paying for any of his initiatives. As a result president Obama faced the recession without the reserves a more cautious, should I say conservative, predecessor might have provided.

Once the banking system stabilized, president Obama was still faced with a serious recession marked by lost equity in housing, credit contractions, and extraordinary job loss. He attempted a traditional Keynesian stimulus which required temporary increases in debt to bolster a flagging economy until the private sector could recover. Some thought the stimulus was insufficient given the depth of the recession, some do not believe in government stimulus at all. I believe that the stimulus worked but not nearly well enough.

What troubles me now is a vague feeling that I am not sure why the stimulus did not work well enough. Perhaps Paul Krugman and other Keynesians are right to insist that the stimulus was insufficient for the depth of the recession. I certainly hope they are right. Or, maybe this is like other credit crunch recessions which typically take 7 to 10 years before recovery. But, I can't help thinking that we are facing something entirely new in the world of economics that leaves any traditional solution or explanation wanting. Emerging markets are blossoming, leaving traditional economies like ours, gasping. Our workers compete with workers all over the world, and we have less and less control over what comprises fair labor practices and fair wages. International regulation of business practices has fallen way behind business acumen in exploiting the opportunities global reach provides.

Deep down I worry about the consumption that drives all economies. Can the rest of the world really consume like developed countries have been consuming without consuming the planet we share? All those emerging economies represent amazing new markets viewed from an economic perspective. What do they represent from an environmental perspective if they consume as we have consumed?

What Next Obama?

November 12, 2008

I've never been conservative about much, but about the federal debt, sometimes I wonder just how we can ever pay for what we've racked up over years of often questionable spending and misdirected tax breaks, and of course I'm not alone. I guess growing up after the generation that survived the great depression, with the survivors as our role models, probably has something to do with the nervousness my generation feels when our leaders throw around the notion of trillions of dollars or so as an acceptable level of debt. Even a titan of the moneyed world, Ted Turner, expressed real concern about it when interviewed on GMA recently.

Economic experts try to ease our concerns by measuring national debt as a percentage of GDP, and they have a point. We know that our own mortgages represent an acceptable level of debt if we have the steady yearly income to pay the interest and some principle while still paying for other necessities and maybe even a few pleasures. GDP stands in the rough analogy for yearly income[87], so a measure that includes debt relative to yearly income (or GDP) makes simple sense. It's certainly better than an unrelated figure like the trillions of dollars or like the often mentioned, yearly federal deficit, which is merely an addition to the overall debt.

A quick web search for federal debt as a percentage of GDP will get you at least one wrinkle and some information intended

---

[87] Actually this analogy is somewhat deceptive. Obviously the government doesn't receive the whole GDP as income. But, the GDP does provide the base for the government's income and the GDP does allow for comparisons with other countries without accounting for different taxing policies.

to be encouraging. You'll find charts that put the percentage of debt to GDP at around 37% and others that put it near 70% or so. An economist actually might be able to make more sense of the differences than I can; all I could find on a government site was an explanation of a total government debt (the 70% figure) and the two components of that total—debt held by the public (the 37% figure) and debt held by one agency of the government and owed by another. Most charts accept the 37% figure, so maybe they think of debt held by the public as the only real debt owed by the government as a whole and the other component as a wash. I must admit to a touch of nervousness about such accounting, but I'll go with the 37%.

So why is 37% of GDP an encouraging level of debt? Other charts show that in terms of US historical percentages, 37% is not too bad. After WWII the percentage was 110%.[88] In other words we owed more than our yearly GDP. Stretching the strained mortgage analogy a bit, that would be like supporting a mortgage of $110,000 with a yearly salary of $100,000. Actually, even that's not so bad. And, of course, the federal government had good reasons for running up such a debt; we'd just fought an all out war, and we'd finally pulled ourselves entirely out of the 30's depression by producing and paying for materials for that war. That percentage went down quite quickly, really, over the next 20 years only to begin rising again under that master of finance, Ronald Reagan. He increased the percentage without a major conflict in part by creating an outsized fear of one with the Soviet Union. There's a drop under Clinton in his last four years (the budget surplus helped) and an increase under the current administration, but none of these fluctuations come anywhere near 110%.

I saw one chart that compared the current 37% US figure to that of other countries. It's sort of encouraging, too, if you like company. We compare with most European countries and actually

---

[88] http://www.whitehouse.gov/omb/budget/fy2008/sheets/hist07z1.xls, actual figures 108 (1946) and 37 (2006). I rounded a bit as have others.

look great when compared to Japan's 100% debt to GDP ratio. We can feel further encouraged about the federal debt if we note one area where the personal mortgage vs. federal debt analogy breaks down. The federal government gets to print extra money,[89] a neat trick they discourage if we try it ourselves. They can pay their debt by printing extra money and then paying it off in inflated dollars. Their ability to print more money or not gives them some control over the level of inflation; we are simply either victimized by it, if our income is fixed, or share in the benefit, if we too are paying off our debt in inflated dollars. Of course the government has to watch out that it doesn't overdo inflation, but the control over it they do have would seem to be a net plus.

Those who would encourage us to accept more debt make the above arguments about the current state of our government's financial affairs. I must admit that their arguments have had the desired effect on my own comfort level—except, except.... Wouldn't you know there are 'excepts'. Unfortunately, even without bailout plans or stimulus packages, we can be pretty sure the debt side of the equation will increase and that the increase will be substantial. Medicare, Medicaid, and Social Security expenses will increase significantly, and if we actually try to provide insurance for most of the 47,000,000 people (and growing) without it, that will cost our government too. Of course we could throw them all under the bus or else send them to emergency rooms, the Bush solution. But, if we want to be humane, we either raise taxes for these increases or we increase the debt. We'll probably do both.

The GDP is a bit less sure to rise, and even less sure to rise significantly enough to cover the federal debt side of the equation. The government projections call for a gradual decline in the percentage from 37 to 32.1 by 2012. With the debt increasing, as

---

[89] Actually 'printing money' is a misnomer for the interaction between central banks and the Federal Reserve. Our government debt includes a third category called monetized debt which I think is the result of this interaction. Here's one place where we need a simplification or an economist.

we know it will, all the decrease in the percentage will have to come from an increase in GDP. OK, I'd like to believe in their projection and the increased GDP on which it is based, too. After what may be 2 quarters of decreasing GDP, I'd really like to believe in a significant increase in GDP, really I would.

If we are depending on enough of an increase in the GDP to cover the increase in federal debt, we need to be talking about how we are going to do that. The answer I'm hearing is to provide a stimulus package. In fact it seems that there are several varieties of stimulus under discussion. First, there's the one the Bush administration—along with an election, obsessed congress—has already tried. That's to pass out checks in the form of tax rebates to practically everyone and hope that they buy, buy, buy; just the advice Bush gave when asked what the American public could do to support his Iraq war adventure. That bailout didn't work.

A slight variation on the untargeted giveaway would stimulate the economy and thus increase GDP by targeting the checks to those who actually need them. Under such a plan, we'd increase unemployment insurance, attempt to stem the tide of foreclosures, give breaks to retirees on fixed income and to others with obvious needs, bail out the auto industry, and provide assistance to state and local governments to stem job loss. The financial justification for this plan rests on the notion that people, companies, or governments in immediate need of money will spend money immediately and not save it. Too much saving went on with the original giveaway. Saving has its longer-term virtues but you need spending to provide the quick boost to the GDP that we need now.

The final stimulus idea introduces something pure free market economists abhor. Not only would we target the stimulus where it is needed financially, we would target what would give us the greatest long-term value. Once you introduce the notion of a government determining what has long-term value, you leave the unfettered market folks behind. For them, the whole point is that the market through pricing determines value, nothing else. A high-heeled shoe has the same value as a solar panel, as long as someone is willing to pay the same price for the shoe as the panel. Well, as I've argued before, it's high time to leave such restrictive notions of value behind.

We have come to the point in our sense of what we value to agree on at least a few long term values we should be willing to support with stimulus money. We value sustainable energy. Both T. Bone Pickens and Ted Turner agree, and they are not wild-eyed, tree-hugging, liberal idealists like me. Government stimulus money spent to develop sustainable energy creates new jobs and therefore stimulates the economy while helping to show the world how to move forward in what many see as a race for survival. That's what I call a two for one bang for the buck. If we apply this realistic, value-oriented approach to the auto industry bailout, then we don't simply give them or loan them money to save jobs and increase GDP. We provide money to retool their industry to produce fuel-efficient vehicles. They get what they need, we get a boost to the GDP, and we get something we value. Wow, that would seem to be a three for one.

Investments in sustainable energy are long-term investments; just like a mortgage, the money will be used to develop and build facilities that will last. Our father's generation taught us that if you must go into debt, don't do it for a vacation in the Bahamas, do it for something that will benefit you long term. They were right about that. Other long-term investments that we should value include education and infrastructure, the two main targets of the recent Chinese stimulus package, incidentally.

Education should include a ramp up in training for the medical personnel we'll need, if we actually do intend to provide real care for an extra 47,000,000 people or so. Infrastructure should include power transmission facilities in order to allow wind and solar energy developed in scarcely populated areas to reach the population centers where the power is needed.

Unfortunately, value oriented, long-term investments don't necessarily provide the immediate boost most economists seem to believe we need now. So what's next Obama? Well, first we need to convince the public that we really are facing a crisis worthy of an increase in the federal debt. The crisis is not comparable to World War II, but we are not asking for an increase in the debt to GDP ratio that's comparable either. The public needs this perspective on what we are doing, and we need someone like you to tell us the facts and to allay lingering fears about debt.

It's time for a radio chat or the current equivalent. Lay out the facts about debt and the principles you will follow for any bailout. What we don't need is another president who increases the debt behind our backs. Trust us. Short term we need to deal with the fallout from the crisis—we need extended unemployment benefits, aid to help those attempting to absorb increased heating bills, and foreclosure aid, now. Even our banks are beginning to see the advantage of foreclosure aid; jump on that good sense.

Next, emphasize the connections between economic interventions and job increases, increases in the GDP, and long-term values. The auto industry bailout we hear that you are discussing provides a perfect illustration of all these connections. There are 3 to 5 million jobs at stake, cars built here could provide a powerful boost to GDP, and having those workers now at risk employed and able to spend more while fearing job loss less, will help too. Finally, we will value the fuel-efficient cars[90] and your advocacy for them, as long as you stick to your guns by insisting that government money go toward developing and building them.

---

[90] I had to add a proposal made in the Wall Street Journal by Paul Ingrassia (former Detroit Bureau Chief of that paper), picked up from Thomas Friedman, NY Times op-ed , 11/12/2008.

"In return for any direct government aid the board and management [of GM] should go. Shareholders should lose their remaining paltry equity. And a government-appointed receiver—someone hard-nosed and non-political—should have broad power to revamp G.M. with a viable business plan and return it to a private operation as soon as possible. That will mean tearing up existing contracts with unions, dealers and suppliers, closing some operations and selling others and downsizing the company... Giving G.M. a blank check—which the company and the United Auto Workers union badly want, and which Washington will be tempted to grant—would be an enormous mistake."

Financial Bailout

February 14, 2009

Let me get this straight. Most economists seem to agree on one problem with any financial bailout scheme. The bad assets that banks held and leveraged to the hilt are extremely difficult to evaluate, and yet they must be evaluated, if we are to deal with them in any way. A New York Times front-page article (2/2/09) neatly summarized the problem by using one mortgage backed bond as an example. The backing for the bond consisted of 9000 second mortgages used by borrowers who put down little or no money to buy homes. Currently about ¼ of the loans are delinquent and losses on defaulted mortgages are at about 40%, according to the article.

You might think that information about the bond, as detailed as this, would aid in establishing a reasonable evaluation. But, it doesn't. The article states that the financial institution that owns the bond quite naturally evaluates at the high end, 97 cents on the dollar. Standard and Poor's, that marvelous credit agency that once rated this bond AAA, now rates it at 87 cents at the current default rate and 53 cents if defaults double. Investors, however, those who are still willing to fork over cash for these creations of Wall Street, offer 38 cents.

Why such differences, other than the obvious fact that the banks and the investors clearly have an interest in the high and low respectively, and the suspicion that Standard and Poor's estimate isn't independent either after years of demonstrating their AAA biases? Well, as the article points out, based on statements by an S and P director (ho ho), calculations would be relatively simple based on any number of different situations; the problem is that we simply don't know which situation our future holds. Will the recession get deeper, driving up default rates as housing prices go down? Or, not? Or, how much deeper and how far up and how far down? People willing to take the plunge and spend money in the face of this kind of murkiness are the super risk takers offering 38 cents on the dollar, and even they are rare these days.

If the risk takers get their price, the drop in the banks' imaginary assets may cause them to collapse, and we are told that the economy cannot withstand such collapses. In fact, many economists out there tell us the banks are already moribund (zombies), so over extended with debt in these devalued securities that the bad debt dwarfs the banks' real assets. If so, then the trick is not to audit them, not to notice the problem until they can recover.[91] Also, we are told, that the only remaining entity capable of jacking up the price to a point high enough to keep the banks solvent or really to restore their solvency and yet to reduce risk enough and to keep the price low enough to encourage more risk takers to jump into the murky waters is, you guessed it, you and I collectively, through our government. Frankly, I've already taken a bath, and I'm not sure I'm anxious to lose more money or take on more risk as a tax-payer than I have already as a 401 K retiree. Poor Mr. Geithner, if he has to convince me to trust this new government to risk the future carefully, imagine what he faces when trying to convince a much more conservative nation. At least he had the guts to tell us the bailout will involve risk, lots of money, and time.

The talking head reaction to Geithner's announced plan has been almost completely negative, and Wall Street dived. The talking heads say they want more detail, though I didn't get a clear idea of what kind of detail they wanted. Did they want Geithner to suggest values for all the convoluted assets out there, or would

---

[91] Some economists claim that this kind of willingness to turn a blind eye cost the Japanese economy 10 years of trouble during the nineties until the prime minister insisted on actually facing the problem. Several European economies have faced the current crisis a lot more directly this time around. See the New York Times business section 2/14/09.

that have been too much detail? Did they want to know what sort of mechanism would be put in place to determine the value of the bad assets? Mechanisms range from letting the market pay what it will (read bank collapse), to government purchase of all the bad assets by creating a US bad bank to hold and eventually sell them (read—"wow, that would make the Bush deficit look cheap"). I think the Geithner plan is somewhere in the middle. Somehow the government sets a bottom price high enough to save the banks but low enough (and with a government guarantee to reduce the risk enough) to entice private capitol to supplement some of the upfront cost. Now that's delicate. Just how much detail for such a complex balancing act would the talking heads like to hear upfront? I've got to say if I were trying to strike such a balance I'd keep as many options open as possible. In fact I'd play it like a poker hand.

As Mr. Geithner probably knew, and is certainly finding out, the problems are not only economic puzzles. He has a public out here upset (to say the least) with Wall Street types who profited obscenely creating a mess and now would like to profit obscenely cleaning it up. And, Mr. Geithner seems to be willing for the sake of saving the economy to let them profit away. Economically that makes sense, but to the American public and to me, it stinks. Attempts to mitigate the public anger center on convincing us that the upfront cost to the government may be only temporary. We would be buying assets, after all, bad now but perhaps better later if we held now and sold later. That's the way we reduced our potential losses from the previous Savings and Loan banking disaster.

The problem seems to be that the upfront costs are simply too high for the public and maybe even the government printing press to endure, hence the desire to include private capitol in the purchasing. Or, at least that's my reading of the tea leaves. So, not only does Mr. Geithner need to work this out so our government doesn't lose too much or risk losing too much, he has to work it out so private risk takers make enough money at a reasonable enough level of risk to encourage them to spend their money now.

Mr. Geithner, economist that he is, has concentrated on the current selling price and risk. But, if he listens to the public, he'll need to think some more about the eventual selling price, or more accurately, about the eventual profit private investors should be allowed to make off the reduced risk they have taken. If he doesn't, he'll bury his party and his president in images of risk takers buying more mega-yachts. So, I'm for setting a limit on their profits. Perhaps we could simply roll another item into the tax code and collect 100% of money made on these instruments over a certain reasonable profit. Or, set up a sliding scale so that as profits increase, taxes increase, until we reach 100%. That almost sounds like a progressive tax, no bipartisan coalition on that sort of radical notion. My feeling? Risk takers deserve profit, but one more yacht on the inland waterway is one more too many for me.

Financial Regulation

June 8, 2009

I remember that Obama campaigners promised to stay active after the election. I'm hoping my own silence over the last several months is not typical. We (the president is gracious enough to include all citizens) need to continue our activity; industry lobbyists certainly haven't let up, though they've been forced to be somewhat more conciliatory or should I just out and out say more devious.

Take those banks we bailed out; they have been forced to agree, at least in principle, that their golden eggs (all those strangely named and oddly constructed derivatives that hatched havoc) need regulation. But trust their greed this far; they don't really want to give up those golden eggs. They need a clever dodge, and you can trust them a couple of steps further; they will come up with one, and they will pay some of the money (that we taxpayers have given them) to their lobbyists and to congressmen in order to ensure that their dodge prevails.

The big bank lobbying organization that citizens need to watch is the recently created CDS consortium[92]. The banks already have a plan, and they are already spending lots of money peddling it. Their plan is simpler than you might expect from creators of collateralized debt obligations (CDO's) or credit default swaps. They seem willing to concede that the trading of those golden instruments needs to be more transparent; all they ask for is one

---

[92] New York Times article 6/1/09. The nine largest derivatives traders created this organization Nov. 13, a month after 5 of its members accepted bailout money, according to the Times article. I rely on this article for most of the information on the lobbyist's strategy.

little loophole that they will be able to drive their Brinks trucks through. What they say they are willing to embrace is the need for some more open trading, like the trading that occurs on a stock exchange.

At least with stock trading people trade openly, knowing the price others are willing to pay, putting buyers in a position to bargain. Seems like capitalism to me. The loophole? The banks want a tiny exception called a "customized swap"—an individualized deal, for flexibility, you understand; not traded openly, you see you do understand. It really is nervy of bankers to insist on trading when the value of the traded object is obscured. Even Milton Friedman would have trouble justifying such a basically anti-capitalist notion.

So, watch for "customized swaps" or anything not traded openly in any bank regulation bill. We'll be back in recession more quickly than the economic cycles would tend to require, if we let the banks buy this ticket to obscene profits. Note that trading in derivatives currently represents transactions with a face value of over $600 trillion up from $88 trillion a decade ago. A decade ago saw the passing of the last piece of conciliatory legislation which allowed the market to explode by exempting derivatives from any real regulation. Imagine what you could rake off the top from a pile of money like that.

If the banks can't get the "customized swaps" loophole, then watch for a subtler, backup plan. The most likely plan would involve trading in a slightly less open arena called a clearinghouse where instead of market based direct trades between buyers and sellers, the trade gets cleared through an intermediary. The N. Y. Times suggests that the clearinghouse[93] likely to be chosen would be regulated, under the Treasury's proposed bill, by The Federal

---

[93] ICE US Trust based in New York City. According to the N. Y. Times article, this clearinghouse has close associations with banks that are members of the CDS Consortium. The Times points out that The Chicago Mercantile Exchange is the more established place for trading derivatives and that it does not have such close ties to the large banks.

Reserve Bank of New York, thought by some critics to be 'too easy on those it oversees'. I'm nervous, however, whenever an intermediary gets involved. I can't help but remember the intermediary function served by the Standard and Poor's ratings of CDO's, the ratings that helped sell those infamous toxic assets. Intermediaries can be influenced (to put it nicely) by interested parties, as S. and P. seems to have been, by sellers of CDO's.

So stay alert. Look for simple and not so simple ploys by banks, insurance companies, lobbyists, our representatives, and, yes, even members of the Obama administration[94]; and then, let your own representative know you see through the ploys. It will help if they know that we know what's going on.

---

[94] Treasury Secretary Geithner, for instance, may support the use of clearinghouses over more open forums for trading derivatives.

CHAPTER 9
Guns

Introduction

The Second Amendment

"A well regulated militia, being necessary to the security of a free state, the right of the people to keep and bear Arms, shall not be infringed."

November, 2011

After the District of Columbia vs. Heller, 5/4 decision established the principle that gun rights extend beyond what I believe is the militia related intent of the second amendment, I promised myself that I would read the court opinion written by Scalia to figure out what went wrong. I ended up reading Scalia's court opinion and the two dissents by Stevens and Breyer. For someone who enjoys carefully reasoned argument, the exercise proved quite engaging.

Scalia is a clever and thorough debater, and reading him first, presented me with arguments I could not refute. One of those arguments had to do with the word 'infringed' in the operative clause. As he points out, the word 'infringed' requires a previous right already established. He refers to the common law individual right to arms and other references to that right as the previously established law 'infringe' must reference. I needed Justice Stevens in dissent to help me counter. Stevens points out that both the individual right to arms and a state's right to a militia existed previously. The one mentioned in the prefatory clause is the militia, so in the absence of any reference to individual rights in the amendment, one should assume that the militia right is the one that must not be infringed. Of course Stevens also argues that 'keep and bear arms' are commonly used terms of the time specific to military and militia activities.

Of particular interest to anyone who enjoys a good debate, are those instances in which both sides refer to the same passages as they did in quoting Pennsylvania's Declaration of Rights of 1776 which said: "That the people have a right to bear arms *for the defence of themselves*, and the state . . . ." Scalia argues that this declaration and Vermont's with similar wording indicate that the two rights were commonly linked. Stevens responds that if they were commonly linked and even specified together in these state bills of rights, then why didn't the writer of the second amendment include this phrasing?

I suppose I could simply continue to be intrigued by Scalia's reasoning and to enjoy Steven's responses if the result of this erroneous decision did not have such severe consequences for public safety. Scalia does his best to limit the damage by insisting that the decision does not negate restrictions on gun use and distribution. Scalia specifically insists that nothing in the ruling should cast doubt on the following prohibitions:

1. Possession of firearms by felons or the mentally ill.
2. The carrying of firearms in sensitive places such as schools or government buildings.
3. Laws imposing conditions and qualifications on the commercial sale of arms.
4. Restrictions on types of weapons.
5. Even the specific trigger lock prohibition he does strike down could easily be allowed by adding another exception to other exceptions already specified in DC's law. Just adding a clause that would allow the removal of the trigger lock in the act of protecting one's home would render the trigger lock prohibition acceptable, according to Scalia. Why he thinks such an obvious point needs to be included rather than assumed baf-

fles me, especially when he includes much less obvious additions to his reading of the second amendment.

Even though Scalia takes the above precautions against over-interpreting restrictions on prohibitions, as Breyer points out, the decision has serious negative consequences. Breyer's reservations deserve quoting: "The decision will encourage legal challenges to gun regulation throughout the Nation. Because it says little about the standards used to evaluate regulatory decisions, it will leave the Nation without clear standards for resolving those challenges....

And litigation over the course of many years, or the mere specter of such litigation, threatens to leave cities without effective protection against gun violence and accidents during that time." Breyer goes on to worry about the effect on future regulation that legislatures might come to believe necessary.

Breyer's prescience struck me today, as I picked up my morning New York Times (11/14/2011). A front page article (with 2 full back pages) chronicled just how lax state laws restricting gun ownership by felons (yes murderers and rapists included) have become. You'd think that even NRA leaders would choke on allowing easy and often largely routine access to legal weapons for those who have used them for serious crimes in their past. Recidivism, after all, is high for major criminals. Perhaps we could consider a delay of 10 years just to see if they intend to do in someone they missed the first time around? But, no, you see once felons serve their time the more radical NRA leaders argue that like other constitutional rights, these people deserve this right as soon as they are released. I suppose free speech or freedom of religion could kill someone, but my bet is that a gun would be more efficacious.

Such blindness to reality is what we have come to expect from those who see only one principle and ignore all others. They are like the blind men determining the nature of an elephant by touching only one part. Each one is quite confident he knows the nature of the beast. All are wrong because none of them can pull back and see the bigger picture. Interestingly enough to mention; in a footnote, Stevens describes Scalia's parsing of the second amendment using the same story. Word by word Scalia argues well, but he misses the big picture that is the subject of this chapter.

Back from Vacation

April 18, 2007

I've got lots of catching up to do. Took a three week camper trip through the south—down the east coast, inland to Atlanta, on down to New Orleans (still in bad shape, except the French Quarter where good drainage into other areas saved the day), up to St Francisville, Miss. (finely preserved antebellum South), then Natchez (home of Creative Marine), Natchez Trace (a favorite of mine), St. Louis, Paducah (quilts as art), Nashville, Gatlinburg, Smoky Mountains, Blue Ridge (another favorite), and then on home through Pennsylvania. Made it back last Thursday in time to prepare for the April 2007 storm of the decade.

Some fine country out there off the interstates, still beautiful dogwoods, redbuds, azaleas, giant rhododendrons (June bloom?) in the Smoky Mountains, well cared for home gardens, preserved Cyprus swamps. I could go on, but I won't. Did finish reading 'Audacity of Hope', Barack Obama, 'Jefferson and the Gun Men', and began 'The Barber of Nashville' (you'll have to look some to find that one). Meanwhile Congress kept busy, I assume; I'll be looking up what went on.

Next day 4/19/2007

Seem to have assumed wrong. Not as much actually accomplished in Congress as I thought might be the case. I guess the military spending bill took up most of the time. Sample—the Native American home loan program (begun in 1996?) was slightly revised, mainly to include native Hawaiians. Ferguson voted against, Holt for, and it passed. I hope to send out a couple of emails today to friends who will know about Native American affairs. Maybe they will let me know about the effect of the loan program on their communities.

Meanwhile the Virginia Tech tragedy unfolds on the news. All I seem to be able to add is a parallel that occurred to me while reading the April 23 edition of Newsweek (out on the stands before Virginia Tech). Paul Dalmas wrote a one page (my turn type) article on the death of his nephew by suicide. This young man had an athletic career in high school, was about to graduate from college in physics, smiled a lot, stood 6' 4", probably had no problem making friends with women, didn't drink or do drugs, came from a loving and supportive family, according to his uncle—and the family and extended family seemed to be close.

The contrast with the Virginia Tech shooter is stark. The shooter never smiled, exuded hate, never talked, obsessed over women, threatened his teachers and classmates; he was everybody's picture of a young man who was likely to be a serious threat to his community. I certainly wonder why a university doesn't seem to have any way to deal with someone like him. One teacher did set up security for herself and her students, but the university itself didn't seem to have any options and still says there was nothing they could do.

Someone ought to think about why our institutions are so paralyzed when confronted with such an extreme profile as the one presented by a young man like the VT shooter. Of course once you go down the profiling path, you'll never reach someone like Paul Dalmas' nephew in time to prevent that tragedy. It's just too buried and subtle. As his cousin said, "(he) was sick, Dad, and he died of the disease." But does that sensible conclusion really mean we can do nothing about troubles writ large like the one at VT?

I don't have any answers to my own questions. So far all I have are some 'couldn't they have' reactions. Thought will have to wait. Couldn't the university have expelled him and prevented him from returning to the campus? Couldn't the FBI have done something useful by keeping an eye on him? Couldn't the university administration have urged the family to seek counseling for him? Was the family even contacted when his English teacher took him out of class and got someone to tutor him privately, because she feared so strongly for her own safety and that of her students? What signals would be sufficient to elicit action of some kind, if these weren't?

And—Virginia's gun laws? Don't get me started on that level of governmental dereliction. OK, so I'm self starting on this one; I'll go into the distorted reading of the 2nd amendment by gun rights advocates, briefly. Last year I read the constitution, the Federalist Papers and some anti-Federalist papers as well as a number of books on the specific issue, in part to understand the 2nd amendment. I'm convinced (as the Supreme Court has been throughout its history) that reasonable restrictions on guns are perfectly within the federal government's jurisdiction.

The 2nd amendment clearly refers to guns related to the maintenance of the militia, and not other guns. Back in those days, guns were very hard to maintain and required central storage and care if they were going to stand a chance of being reliable. Our original government knew enough to ensure the military viability of militia weapons by keeping them out of the hands of untrained individuals. They could do whatever they pleased with their own weapons.[95]

Besides the 2nd amendment debate was part of a larger concern over standing armies, a concern strongly and justifiably felt by many of those American citizens who had just defeated the strongest standing army in the world at the time. They certainly

---

[95] I added this footnote on 11/14/2011 after reading the 2008 Supreme Court decision and dissents for DC vs. Heller, the unfortunate second Amendment ruling. It is true that militia guns were kept in armories, but it is also true as both Scalia and Stevens (in dissent) mention that militia men were required to 'keep' their own arms. Over the years the weapons kept at home became too unreliable, hence the storage in armories. My lack of knowledge about this militia requirement negates what I tried to imply by separating personal guns from militia guns. They could be the same guns, though the right to them referenced in the second amendment should have remained a militia based right.

did not feel at all comfortable giving their own federal government anything like the British regulars.

The framers, though, for the most part, knew what George Washington knew; no militia based force could protect the US for long. The second amendment might be best seen as a sop to the militia myth so strongly felt by the general citizenry, but so clearly understood for what it was by military men like Washington. Let them have their militia, give them guns centrally maintained; it could be of some use, and more important they'll feel a bit better about the standing army we are going to need as soon as we can get one.

Sorry about the digression, but I just can't let a historically inaccurate interpretation of the 2nd amendment stand as our gun policy. I'm afraid that what bolsters the Texas/Virginia form of the NRA argument (we all have some absolute right to run around with guns and should do so) may well be just the sort of government or institutional inaction or paralysis that gripped the VT community prior to the shootings. If our institutions can't protect us, then we need to protect ourselves. That argument surfaced in student interviews. They said if guns weren't banned on campus then we'd have had our guns and we could have done something, maybe. Conservative Republicans like George Wills and Newt Gingrich have echoed these thoughts.

That argument sounds sane enough unless you believe as I do in a much more likely scenario. Guns in the hands of untrained or even trained civilians are much more likely to lead to escalated arguments—what should result in no more than bloody noses or verbal insults escalating into shootouts. Stray bullets hit those uninvolved. That's not my idea of security.

Even trained police offers make serious errors of judgment under pressure. Ask the trainers (often responsible NRA members) how officers do the first time out in fire under pressure exercises. I bet they have stories to tell. We've had some horrendous examples in NYC over the last few years of what happens when

even those who are trained reach the field and actually partici-
pate in an incident. We certainly should not look to amateurs to
do well in such situations. We have institutions to keep us from
resorting to the wild-west, and we need to concentrate on how to
improve their performance.

Fifteen minutes for anyone with a driver's license to buy a
9 mm? That's not responsible government. If you are going to
own guns, some minimum training (I'd opt for vigorous training)
should be part of the deal you make with the rest of us. Responsible members of the NRA try hard to help out here too, incidentally.
Waiting periods and real background checks have to be part of the
deal too. No instant background check system will ever provide
the time for real, thorough checking. The VT shooter passed. You
don't get to use other deadly items like cars without basic protec-
tions for the rest of us, why are guns different?

Would any of these measures have prevented the VT disaster?
Well, a waiting period might have given the university community
more time to react. Perhaps a decent background check might
have included interviews with one of his teachers. Maybe even
the teachers, who did take steps, would have had time to make a
bigger fuss. If the shooter had gotten training from a responsible
gun owner, perhaps something would have come up in training.
He might have developed some sort of relationship that might
have helped, though he seemed incapable of relationships. Maybe
his parents would have known that he was applying for a gun. All
these are maybes, yes, but to my way of thinking, they are better
maybes than a last second chance that someone else on campus
would blast away at him, hit him, and stop further damage, rather
than inflicting collateral damage him or herself.

Compare NJ's gun laws with Virginia's. A Philadelphia reporter
(NJ resident), interviewed on NPR went through our handgun permit procedure. It took 8 weeks and 6 days. There were interviews.
Spouses needed to be informed. Good to know when your spouse
is getting a gun. The police department conducted interviews

with the applicant. Sounds to me like the opportunity to stop the VT shooter ahead of time would have been improved if all states adopted NJ gun laws, or if we had similar national requirements. Without the participation of all states or national laws, it's too easy to go to Virginia or Pennsylvania and get your 15 minute 9 mm.

So where are the Democratic politicians this time around? Republicans, except some big city mayors, seem hopelessly tied to the political arm of the NRA. Responsible NRA members don't seem to control their leaders. So, let's get on our congressmen about gun control. Here's a test for your congressman. What did he or she do when the Tiahrt amendment passed the neo-conservative congress of 2003? The Tiahrt amendment restricts law officers from sharing gun identification information for guns used in crimes. That's right, guns used in crimes. Admittedly the ATF (Bureau of Alcohol, Tobacco, Firearms (and Explosives)) funding buried in Department of Justice Appropriations to which the amendment was attached was complex, but if my congressman had anything to do with that amendment, I'm sure I couldn't vote for him. Maybe congress will separate the amendment from the funding, and rescind it. Seems the least we should be asking. I'm going to write Ferguson, my representative, on this one.

Representative Mike Ferguson Responds

May 13, 2007

I had promised to write my Republican congressman Mike Ferguson to find out his views on repealing the 2003 Tiahrt amendment. See previous blog entry on gun control. Here's his response:

Thank you for contacting me regarding gun-violence prevention. I appreciate hearing from you and having the benefit of your views.

As the father of four young children, I believe Congress should take common-sense steps to keep firearms out of the hands of criminals and children. In the House, I have consistently voted to uphold gun-violence prevention laws and opposed efforts that would weaken those laws.

For example, I support reinstating the now-expired assault weapons ban, support closing the gun-show loophole, support expanding the National Instant Criminal Background Check System, and voted to uphold the firearm ban in the District of Columbia.

In an effort to combat illegal gun trafficking, I support legislation creating new federal penalties for criminals who use stolen firearms with concealed serial numbers during the commission of a felony. The issue of gun trafficking is particularly important to New Jersey because the majority of guns used in crimes in the state illegally cross New Jersey's borders.

In 2005, I voted to restrict gun manufacturers' exports of high-powered, .50-caliber rifles that can bring down jet airliners from a mile away. In 2007, I became a founding member of the Congressional Taskforce Against Illegal Guns, which was established to help law enforcement gain the tools it needs to combat gun-related crimes and the illegal trafficking of firearms.

I will remain a strong advocate in Congress of common-sense legislation to keep guns out of the hands of criminals and children.

Again, thank you for taking the time to share your opinions with me and please visit my website at www.house.gov/Ferguson for more information on issues important to New Jersey's 7th Congressional District.

Lots of positive support from my congressman here. Most important—he says he supports closing the gun show loophole. He doesn't specifically address the Tiahrt Amendment unless you interpret his participation in the Congressional Taskforce against Illegal Guns a response. We'll have to wait and see if the taskforce leads to a repeal of the amendment.

Meanwhile there was at least one sane move in response to the VT event. The Governor of Virginia has acted by insisting that someone who is mentally ill and so dangerous to himself and others as to warrant involuntary in-patient or out-patient care should be included in the background database for those requesting gun permits.

Of course as I stated in my previous entry, I do not believe any instant check, no matter how complete the database claims to be, is sufficient. One wonders if those who believe in the importance of medical information privacy will join the guns for all folks in resisting any inclusion of medical information in a national database. They would have some fairly good reasons for requiring extreme caution, but in this case I'd hope they would all think carefully about tradeoffs.

The Second Amendment

"A well regulated militia, being necessary to the security of a free state, the right of the people to keep and bear Arms, shall not be infringed."

February 11, 2008

This entry is something of a note to me on gun control, a topic I've addressed in previous entries. I'd argued that strict constructionists, including those on the Supreme Court, who most often make the claim to be strict constructionists, would need to deal with the militia clause of that amendment in any interpretation. In order to do so, they would need to consider the historical context of that clause.

I'd argued that any reader of documents written at the time (including the Federalist and Anti-Federalist papers) could hardly avoid understanding that the militia discussion was directly related to our founding fathers' quite natural fear of standing armies. The new nation had just defeated the most powerful standing army in the world, and the newly enfranchised citizens were not anxious to concede the power of a standing army to a yet to be tested, central, governmental authority. Broaden the context a bit further, and the issue becomes a classic question of state rights vs. federal rights, state militias vs. a federal standing army.

Our founding fathers most familiar with military tactics of the day, George Washington among them, had a difficult political problem on their hands. They knew that developments in military weapons and tactics required that the US maintain a standing army (and navy for that matter), but they also knew that the country had a deep love of citizen militias, in fact a love so deep that it bordered on mythic attachment. The 2nd amendment solved the political problem by clearly recognizing the rights of state militias to bear arms, and in return for this guarantee, those who opposed standing armies allowed the federal government to determine its own military needs without the specific constitutional prohibition they favored. For those who love detail, there is a prohibition against funding the army for longer than two years without reauthorization by congress.

Recently I stumbled across further evidence of this bargain in Al Gore's <u>Assault on Reason</u>. Thomas Jefferson, commenting on the first draft of the constitution sent to him by James Madison, insisted on attaching a bill of rights including the following 5 items:

"1. Religion shall be free; 2. Printing presses free; 3. Trials by jury preserved in all cases; 4. No monopolies in commerce; 5. No standing army." Number 5 was unacceptable to military authorities of the time, but Jefferson and company needed something. They got a guarantee that their militias would remain intact, written as a constitutional right, a right so important to them that it is included by Jefferson up there with four others we all (with the exception of our current president) understand as critical. That militias have the absolute right to bear arms may no longer seem important to us, but the historical changes that make this right to state militias obsolete should have nothing to do with a strict constructionist view of the constitution.

We may see something about just how strict Alito, Roberts, and Thomas really are when 2nd amendment issues come before the court sometime this summer (I think). Will they even consider the militia clause and the standing army history behind it, or will they capitulate to the current reading made popular by private gun ownership advocates? If the amendment refers to militias, as I believe the introductory clause and historical documents strongly indicate, then it says nothing about private gun ownership, leaving those issues to congressional action. That has been the prevailing

Supreme Court decision so far. Gun laws are legal, not prevented by the 2nd amendment. Federal gun laws already exist.

What we should be debating is how restrictive the laws ought to become. Should the federal government insist on improving instant gun registration checks by licensed gun dealers so that madmen like the Virginia Tech killer might have to go elsewhere for guns? Should those checks extend to gun shows where the Columbine killers got their guns? Should there be multiple checks extended over months, as the law in New Jersey requires, or are instant checks sufficient? Should the laws be federal, so those who wish to avoid New Jersey's laws can't head across the border to Pennsylvania or south to Virginia? These questions are the ones we need to address.

We may see if the current court decides to legislate by itself by ignoring the introductory clause of the second amendment, constitutional history, and the established interpretation in order to pass into law the politically favored, national gun lobby view. Or, if maybe they will decide finally, with sufficient clarity, to interpret the 2nd amendment strictly, allowing real gun law discussions to occur in the political arena, free from pseudo-appeals to a misinterpretation of the 2nd amendment. I guess I'm not going to hold my breath for anything quite that clear; I'd settle for some mention of the history in a strict constructionist majority opinion.

Give Me Liberty, No Wait, Give Us an Army

March 19, 2008

I've written several entries on the second amendment, and now the Supreme Court is about to take up the issue, some 69 years after its last attempt. Newsweek this last week had a single page piece on the subject by Dahlia Lithwick 'When Reason Meets Rifles'. The article referred to a Liberal/ Libertarian line of thought that seemed to me to be one more example of the way fervid ideology prevents those who ought to know better from understanding what ought to be obvious. I couldn't help responding by trying my hand at one of those horribly condensed letters to the editor. Sound bites aren't my style; I like to chew over my thoughts more slowly—but here it is anyway.

Dahlia Lithwick mentions a liberal/libertarian reading that places the 2nd amendment in the context of the constitution's general respect for individual rights. However, the clear context for the second amendment is the founders' quite legitimate fear of standing armies, not the question of liberty. The citizens of the time had just defeated, at great cost, a powerful standing army, and they did not want to establish another, even if it was nominally their own. Thomas Jefferson, writing to James Madison on the first draft of the constitution, insisted on a bill of rights including five items, four familiar today and the fifth 'No standing army'. Military men of the time knew full well what Jefferson did not want to acknowledge, that the country would not survive relying on state militias alone without a standing army. Think of the second amendment as an astute political compromise—loyal state citizens get their beloved state militias enshrined as a constitutional right; the nation gets the army it will soon need.

CHAPTER 10
Final Thoughts

Introduction

2/7/2013

A few final thoughts came to me after publishing the first edition, so I've tagged them on here and called the result the second edition. A bit too often, I find myself repeating the same basic ideas and even some of the same studies as documentation, but also I find that the same issues remain a part of our political discussion and that opposing positions seem to me to remain as immune from any reliable evidence as ever.

I was dragged back into the fray by a couple of editorials in local newspapers, but I must admit that once I got started again, stopping was not easy. I hope the cure to this addiction came when I finished the entry entitled 'Postscript'. That blog entry was an attempt to think beyond politics, not a new thought either, but perhaps an appropriate period to a series of political blogs.

Letter to the Editor

5/9/2012

I was intrigued by a fellow citizen's letter to the editor (May 2012), not because I haven't heard his supply side, generally neo-conservative arguments before but because his concise expression of those arguments so clearly revealed where my fellow Belle Mead resident and I disagree. He attacked our representative, Leonard Lance, for supporting two of the very few issues where our representative and I agree or did agree–funding 'The Affordable Health Care Act ' and passing Cap and Trade. I'm fairly sure our representative is not emphasizing either vote in his current campaign.

Back in March 2010 Representative Lance granted me a half hour interview in which we discussed our differences. I centered the discussion on issues we both saw as critical but which we prioritized differently. My representative has made the debt his primary concern, fairly consistently; but I think the debt is a far less significant legacy we will leave to our grandchildren than an unsustainable environment, an unhealthy public, and an educational, global advantage on the decline.

During my interview with Representative Lance I buttressed my fiscal arguments by recalling Milton Friedman's elegant definition of value–which could be simplified as what the public will pay balanced against the cost of production. If the cost of production goes too high, the public will no longer pay the price, and the producer will need to adjust in whatever way possible, including by going out of business, or more creatively, by inventing a new, less expensive product–the mechanical pencil to replace the cedar, lead/graphite predecessor product, for instance.

All I did in my argument with Representative Lance was to suggest a 21st century update to the definition of value, adjusting the cost of production side in order to account more rigorously for the societal costs of producing objects. These days all of us should realize that we need to pay for the environmental costs of production, and I'd add we need to pay for the moral costs. Child labor in factories and slavery are two very efficient and all too common 21st century ways of reducing the cost of production, but most of us would find both immoral. Think of the recent Apple/Chinese labor issue as another example. Apple products will cost more if Apple management really insists on anything like humane labor conditions at their Chinese plant.

My fellow citizen (and despite the 'lapses' he noted probably Representative Lance), consistent with their shared priorities, support or tend to support tax reduction on those they consider society's producers. Flat taxes, business tax reductions, elimination of the inheritance tax, keeping capital gains and dividend taxes low–all derive from a belief that our fundamental problem is debt resulting from government spending on non-producers and that the answer to that debt is tax reduction on the producers.

I would like to join my fellow citizen in suggesting a more efficient tax, but one consistent with my priorities instead of his. Let's introduce a Value Added Tax (VAT), but let's call it the Value Adjusted Tax. The tax would be administered like the traditional VAT (each producer in the production chain receiving credit for checking that the previous producer paid their tax), but we could think of it as an adjustment in the price of products for the environmental costs of production and the moral costs of production. Incidentally, VAT's an efficient, less complicated tax. Coupled with a simplified income tax, it might well go a long way toward handling our debt and our need to foster future producers, perhaps even some future producers currently of less than stellar means. We might even take care of our veterans, send more of our population on to college, and improve our infrastructure. Such investment is both productive and moral.

Response to Letter to the Editor

5/25/2012

I had wanted to question more of the points made by my fellow citizen's letter to the editor published in a local paper (May 2012), but newspapers do have space concerns, and actually talking about issues takes way more space than simply stating preconceived conclusions. So, I'll take up another issue here.

Many conservative Republicans have convinced themselves that increased state income taxes on high income earners drives these productive citizens to migrate to other states, taking their talents and tax creation potential with them. As my fellow citizen puts it, in reference to New Jersey, "we have witnessed the outward migration to other states of our best producers." Another similarly minded citizen, in another local paper, a week or so later, made the same point, stating among other 'horrors' that "if you want more businesses and high earners that actually pay taxes to leave the state" then elect Democrats.

Fortunately there have been studies of the 2004 New Jersey tax increases that addressed this notion of increased migration due to increased state tax rates. When I wrote about this about a year ago I cited a Princeton University study of high earner migration after the 2004 New Jersey tax increase on high earners (an increase from 6.37% to 8.97% on income above $500,000). The study found "little impact" on high income earner migration. The tax raised the state's income by more than a billion dollars in 2006 against a loss of 37.7 million dollars from migration or a loss of less than 3.7% of the gain.[96] Apparently, high income earners in large numbers stayed and paid. Few fled to avoid being bled.

---

[96] 'Trends in New Jersey Migration: Housing, Employment, and Taxation' By Christobal Young, Charles Varner, and Douglas S. Massey

Of course studies often turn off those with pre-conceived notions, and they are likely to find, somewhere, another study that supports their views. In fact there are studies that take total migration out of New Jersey and then imply that high earners follow the same patterns. Other studies rely on anecdotal replies from selected respondents where the selection criteria are highly suspect. One such badly designed study is often all someone already convinced needs.

I'm finding that sometimes a simpler discussion may get through where a complex study doesn't. So let's just look at what you or I might do if we were faced with a tax increase on our $500,000 taxable income. So many of us face this dreadful situation each year that I'm sure you won't have to put on your magic caps to imagine the situation you'd face. First, note that the tax increase applies only to income over $500,000. So let's up our income to $700,000 and see just how painful the increased tax would be. For ease of calculation we can calculate the damage of 1% and then you can calculate the 2.6% for the 2004 increase.

Here's a chart from a Rutgers study[97] with someone making slightly less than the low end of a teacher's salary range thrown in for comparison.

High Income Surcharge (1%) on taxpayers with Income over $500,000

	Tax Payer A	Tax Payer B
Income	$40,000	$700,000
Current tax	$1,600	$41,200
Additional tax:		
Income over $500,000	0	$200,000
Times .01=surcharge	0	$2,000
Total tax w/surcharge	$1,600	$43,200

---

[97] See Center on Budget and Policy Priorities, 'Raising State Income Taxes on High-Income Taxpayers' By Elizabeth McNichol, Andrew Nicholas, and Jon Shure

OK, so now stretch your imagination a bit more and think what a burden $2,000, or $4,000, or $6,000 more off your taxable income would be. Go ahead and really blow yourself out of the water and say your tax is now $50,000. Perhaps you missed or miscalculated a deduction or two. With a miserable $650,000 of taxable income left, would you leave your job in perhaps the high end financial industry or pharmaceutical industry, leave some of the nation's best schools, leave friends, business acquaintances, and suppliers, leave behind a hard earned, local business reputation? And, you would move where? Go ahead and sell your house into a lousy market, pay your first couple of year's savings on moving expenses, and then try finding an equivalent salary or business opportunity in some low tax state with schools to match.[98] If such a move makes sense to you, then, please, explain your thinking to me as simply as possible so I can understand.

Incidentally, the Princeton University study, mentioned above, notes that those earning $500,000 or more increased in number 70% between 2002 and 2006 despite the 2004 tax increase. So, if we do lose a few through migration, we way more than make up for the tiny loss in state revenue due to migration by being an economically vibrant area. We can afford to remain vibrant by spending increased taxes on the education, infrastructure, and research that help make New Jersey such a profitable place to live.

---

[98] NY Times, 2/7/13, article on California state tax increases that raised the state plus federal income taxes for millionaires above 50% made some of the same points.

Healthcare Debate?

7/7/2012

What's going on? Television, newspapers, pundits claim to be talking about 'The Affordable Healthcare Act', but what I hear repeated ad nauseum is whether the act includes a tax or a penalty. I can't imagine a less productive debate. It's both, folks; and yes, taxes are necessary, and if well spent, a good thing. So, let's get on to talking about the act itself, and let's do that by talking about whether it moves us forward toward a better healthcare system. What a novel idea.

To figure out whether it moves us forward, we need to look back in order to sketch out what we had before the bill passed. I got some important insights into our unique health insurance system yesterday by listening to Brian Lehrer's NPR interview with guest Robert H. Frank, New York Times columnist and Cornell economics professor. At its base, our healthcare insurance system relies on the workplace. No other country saddles businesses with the burden of insuring workers, so how come we do?

Dr. Frank traces this anomaly back to WWII. He says that we decided to pay workers and soldiers at something like the same rates, even though businesses were starved for industrial labor and willing to pay much more. We just couldn't stomach paying soldiers risking their lives really low wages while paying those who stayed home a much higher going rate. Paying the soldiers more, bolstering our allies with supplies, fighting a war, replacing equipment, we couldn't do it all; so, we passed a law capping wages for workers at home. OK, one could argue, that's roughly fair; after all, at that time, we believed in the old-fashioned notion of shared sacrifices. But, businesses still needed workers, and the lowered salaries weren't bringing them in fast enough. So, creative businesses added another draw, an unregulated one no one had thought about, free health insurance.[99]

---

[99] The idea clearly caught on during the war years. In 1940 9% of workers were covered by employers, by 1953 that figure reached 63%. Brian Lehrer Interview

What an odd set of circumstances Dr. Frank relates as the origins for our employer based health insurance system. Why would we insist on keeping this stop-gap system permanently? Faced with a global economy, our industrial base can't really afford the extra cost, while their competitors in other countries are blessed with more inclusive systems to cover the population's medical costs.

Many of our companies, feeling the growing competition, are finding ways to remove this albatross or at least lessen its drag. Policies get skimpier, workers share more of the premium increases, labor unions take on the burden, and more and more companies simply drop it or rely on temps or contractors who don't get company insurance. Why wouldn't those self appointed protectors of business, Republicans, jump at the chance to help companies shed this burden?

When the 'Affordable Healthcare Act' exchanges kick in (2014), we'll hear more from opponents, particularly Republicans, about how businesses are taking the easy out by dropping health insurance policies and dumping employees on the exchanges. We're already hearing exactly that argument from them. I found Dr. Frank's response to that possibility particularly refreshing. Good, he said, the quicker employer based insurance fades the better. It's a bad idea for today's world.

Indeed, employer based health insurance is a bad idea in today's world. Employers get it. Already coverage of the employed has dropped from a high of 75% to today's low of 55%, according to Dr. Frank. Creative arguments will crop up claiming that it's all because of the healthcare law exchanges, but let's just ignore such speculative logic. The real business sense reasons are here now and so obvious one has to wonder about the motives of those who blame exchanges that don't even exist yet.

Workplace based health insurance burdens companies, and I'd argue that it burdens workers too. Forget about the fact that

with Dr. Frank.

it's getting less reliable and more expensive. It's tied to work, and when workers lose jobs they eventually lose insurance too, after COBRA runs out or sooner if they can't pay the exorbitant COBRA insurance rate.

I've argued before that pensions tied to one employer are bad for employees because they tie the employee to one company whereas successful employment these days, more and more often, means moving around. People change employers often now and they even change careers. Liberated employees free to adjust quickly to changing market demands will succeed in the future, and they will do so more easily if their retirement savings and their health insurance become equally flexible. Moveable 401 K's rolled into IRA's need to replace pensions and exchange based insurance or some other evolution of healthcare insurance needs to replace the anachronism that employer based insurance has become.

We'll have to see if the exchanges really do improve care and cut costs within a framework that most agree is fair. That framework now includes a few simply stated principles that most support. Insurance companies cannot deny coverage based on pre-existing conditions. They cannot limit yearly outlay or life-time outlay for those among the insured who are unfortunate enough to become seriously ill. We'll see if the open market place provided by the exchanges can reduce medical costs by spawning the creativity that profit and markets are supposed to encourage within a fair framework.

In order to remain profitable, insurance companies may find that they need to change payment practices from fee for service to results-based medicine, or they may find that healthcare provid-ers like Kaiser Permanente and the Mayo clinic, highly successful organizations that handle business issues themselves by paying staff including doctors salaries and by paying malpractice claims outright, end up becoming winning entries on the exchanges.

In previous blogs I've supported both results based medicine and larger business entities as better medical delivery models, and Dr. Frank mentioned these possibilities too, adding that some creative solution we haven't even thought about might emerge. Republicans who support the profit motive, even in the medical field where many find that motive questionable, should be excited about the potential for creative, market based solutions. After all, we've adopted their approach with just a few humane regulations. If they can't live with this very American compromise, I wonder what they can accept.

Postscript

Political campaigns and too many of the news outlets that report on them blind us to longer term trends; they strive for immediate effects, and they tend to blur any meaningful discussion of what our future might become. What's the jobless rate, now? What will it be before the election? Consideration of how the Affordable Healthcare Act might turn out, once implemented in 2013/2014, seems sketchy at best. Apparently it's a stretch to make a campaign issue out of what such a major change might be like only one or two years from now.

Some issues, like the debt or Medicare funding shortfalls, do draw campaigns into making what are almost always gloomy predictions about the future, too often meant to scare us into one position or another. But, I'd argue that political discussion of these issues remains grounded in very narrow visions. Politicians seem more comfortable taking a view of the future that differs very little from their public's prevailing view of the present. Perhaps they have to in order to appeal and win. To really consider our future as a country we need to break out of campaign mode and ask questions that our politicians and most of the rest of us are unlikely to ask in the heat of the election season and even after, given the media's obsession with current events.

Let's look at jobs; we all seem to agree—job creation is a central issue. Republican candidates decry the 8.x% jobless rate and add that even this unacceptable rate is low because it doesn't account for those who have 'given up' looking. Democratic candidates point to the slightly more recent 7.8% or 7.9% rate and emphasize that at least we are back creating jobs, but that the rate of job creation, though moving in the right direction, is insufficient and that the number who have given up is disturbing.

Both parties trot out their own predictable solutions– increasing growth through decreased taxes at the top or encouraging private enterprise through targeted tax breaks or supporting state and local governments or pushing ahead with infrastructure improvements or stimulating demand by giving tax breaks to middle income earners and subsidies to the poor (both these groups more likely than the upper 1% to spend money immediately). Anyone who has been listening can fill out the scripts.

A number of slightly more thoughtful commentators have pointed to several longer term, job depressing factors not mentioned often enough, if at all, by politicians. We gained many, many, good manufacturing jobs because our president saved GM, Chrysler, and their parts suppliers by investing government money. That's good, but few politicians seem willing to mention that there are far fewer jobs in auto manufacturing and manufacturing in general than there used to be and that the downward trend may well continue. They all seem to believe that manufacturing will recover if only we follow this policy or that one.

One reason for the decline is obvious–automation; robots make humans doing manual work much less necessary. US workers lose out to robots, but apparently more worthy of news coverage, they lose out to foreign workers. Globalization and relatively inexpensive worldwide transportation mean most products can be manufactured more economically elsewhere and then shipped here for less than we can make them. All we hear from politicians is how unfair trade practices have become, not what global companies so clearly know–that automation, globalization, and improved transportation make perfectly good business sense, even though they may cost American manufacturing jobs. And, as consumers, the rest of us like the lower prices.

Fewer manufacturing jobs would be bad enough news, but it is not the only area where job shrinkage is occurring. An Oct. 5 article in the NY Times chronicles some less than encouraging trends in what should be our economy's sweet spot–small, innovative, startup company employment. These companies are beginning to realize that as startups they do better by hiring consultants rather than full time employees. Consultants often don't get paid benefits and they are not organized, but perhaps even more important for startups, consultants provide flexibility as the need for the new products either surges or plunges. Dropping consultants in slow times and then rehiring them when business picks up is relatively easy. Even established companies have been catching on.

The NY Times article mentioned yet another area for actual and potentially increasing job loss. Back office activities of all sorts now get farmed out to companies that have sprung up to handle these issues. The ADP concept of handling other companies' payroll tasks can expand to include many other tasks not directly related to a particular company's main business. Startups may be especially creative in farming out this kind of work, but the concept certainly has the potential of expanding more widely beyond startups to companies in general. Such back office consolidation leads to just what the word 'consolidation' implies–a reduction in the number of employees needed overall.

Paul Krugman came up with one potential balancing trend to the job loss trends (Oct. 8 NY Times editorial). The number of adults within the prime, employment age range is decreasing as more and more baby boomers retire and leave the work force. This change means that the number of jobs required to keep up with the work age population is decreasing, and I assume this trend will continue for a while, even if we attempt to balance the trend by allowing increased immigration of young workers. Of course us oldsters might well support increased legal immigration and might wish that jobs could keep up with a larger number of workers so their contribution to payroll taxes could help pay for our hard earned benefits.

Businesses improve the bottom line whenever they drop non-essential employees, and they thrive when they are creative in doing so. Governor Romney knows this simple fact; he built a business on it. Perhaps we need to acknowledge the possibility that businesses will succeed quite well and that as a consequence the ratio between available jobs and workers in the US will worsen no matter what our politicians do and no matter how demographics might alter the pool of workers.

What do we do about the jobs issue if we make the not completely unreasonable assumption that lost manufacturing jobs, consulting instead of full time employment, and back office consolidation really do lead to fewer available jobs and if we assume that immigration of young workers will negate much of the decline in the work age population?

A few figures might help alert us to what I've come to see as related 21st century realities. In 2011 US population represented about 4.7% of world population. For the sake of comparison, China comes in at 19.15%, India at 17.2%, and Indonesia at 3.78%. And yet, by a couple of different measures (world GDP and Purchasing Power Parity) the US consumes 20% or so of what the world produces. We consume 24% of the world's energy.

The disparity between population numbers and consumption was possible in the 20th century. In fact, it existed in even starker terms if we can believe a figure I saw for the western world circa 1912. Apparently, then, the western nations (including the US) consumed 80% of the world's output. According to Niall Ferguson such 20th Century dominance by the west in general dates back some 600 years, and it is based on a set of what he calls the West's six wealth producing "apps"–political and economic competition, the scientific revolution, the rule of law, modern medicine, education, and the work ethic. Unfortunately these apps are no longer so entirely ours alone. The trends over the last few decades are disturbing; in too many of these western apps, the US is falling behind and/or others are catching up.

If we simply thought along current lines, we might envision any number of future horrors or possibilities. Economists might limit their thinking to–either 'look at all those new consumers', or to 'look at all those new competitors', or to both responses. Environmentalists might focus on consumption and sum up the results as I have once or twice or..., imagining, for instance, a Hummer in every Chinese garage. That thought might even cause a Republican or two to open their eyes and noses to the environmental consequences of rampant, US style, global consumption. Both the economic and the environmental views contain kernels of truth for politicians to exploit, but both views lack the wider vision required to solve US job problems or global consumption problems.

So, back to the question–'what do we do about the possible shortage of US jobs in the 21st century'? Let's begin by noting that since the 1950's the work force in America has increased dramatically. I'm not talking about mere population increases, certainly significant; I'm talking about the immense increase in two earner households. The women's movement brought many more workers into the workforce relatively quickly, and somehow the economy absorbed that increase and thrived. Did it thrive because women were paid less or because salaries in general began to flat-line or because we hit a sweet spot for US businesses?

Maybe that ability to absorb so many new, employable adults should be considered an out of the ordinary period in our history, fueled by an extraordinary consumption binge. And, maybe the current unemployment numbers represent some sort of return to what a normal economy is capable of absorbing in the way of workers. In other words maybe the current unemployment numbers will become our new, 21st century norm. Imagine a politician expressing this possibility. I'm a bit annoyed at myself for thinking such thoughts.

Let's hope politicians are right about the future for once. Let's hope government investment in basic science and in education will help spark the new, innovative industries we will need. Let's hope basic research and development result in the blossoming of new industries we can't even imagine today. Let's hope we don't follow the Romney/Ryan script that calls for cuts in these crucial areas of discretionary, government investment, the source of so many of our current marvels.

We can hope, but perhaps we need to think a bit, too. Do our 20th century ways of thinking about jobs hold up to 21st century realities? Even our ways of collecting jobs data may be 20th century holdovers to some extent, in need of updating. The household survey that establishes the number of unemployed asks two basic questions. Are you out of work? Are you searching for work? Let's consider how the increasing number of consultants might answer those questions. Businesses hire consultants so they can get rid of them easily when business deceases and hire them back when business increases. Consultants, then, by definition almost, are out of work at various times and always looking. The condition 'out of work and looking', might become normal for more and more workers in the 21st century, not the negative that 'unemployed and looking' implies in our current political lingo.

If unemployed becomes more normal, maybe we will need to reconsider the life style and related consumption habits that many of us have come to consider an integral part of our American dream. I've certainly noticed, as I'm sure many others have, that increasing possessions, riches, and even fame do not necessarily have a linear relationship with increasing happiness.

Let's be quite clear here. There is no way the earth can sustain worldwide consumption on the US 20th century model. If the US really wants to be an economic and moral leader in the 21st century, then we need to reconsider 'getting and spending' consumption and focus on what sustainable consumption might look like. When a Hummer sells for $50.00 as scrap metal and a slim book of verse nets $40,000.00, we'll know we're on the right track. Maybe then, job statisticians will begin asking 'does your family income meet your needs' rather than asking whether someone in your family is currently unemployed and looking for a job. And, we'll all get to think about what our 'needs' might be.

Many insist that what we want in the way of jobs to drive our 21st century economy are high skilled, requiring a highly educated pool of workers. These are the jobs that will create the exports we need to balance the imports we consume. They will become the best path to balancing our budget. In terms of pure numbers these jobs probably won't compensate for job losses elsewhere but they will be better jobs for which workers could demand better salaries.

Better salaries might mean that some of those in the earning years, running around struggling to juggle the two earner family model, might be freed to reconsider the single earner model. Some of those freed from the job market (men or women) might make family life a less hectic experience, some might volunteer for activities they really enjoy, some might have time to develop talents too often neglected, some might even become entrepreneurs, leading to jobs for others.

The 20th century really was America's century; we became the financial and industrial powerhouse; we invented what the world came to want. We shined as a democracy that kept expanding, and we convinced ourselves that most of us, if not all of us, shared in the fruits. It was one heady experience; no wonder that we would want to cling to what we came to see as the American dream. But we've entered the 21st century, and we may need to dream anew. We can start by realizing that the jobs problem is not an isolated issue. It's tangled up in a nexus of broader questions about what we want to become and what we want our country to become.

So many opportunities for real improvements stare us in the face–better mass transit, improved urban design, worldwide social networking, better fossil fuel energy sources, non-fossil fuel energy sources–many ways to change our consumption habits, many ways to become a more people oriented society. For starters, education, improved health, and basic research really do need to become the primary goals. And, to pay for improvements, why

261

not drop the antiquated notion that we and we alone have the moral authority to police the world. We should drop that outrageously expensive, amazingly arrogant, 20th century notion like the hot potato it's become and actually always was.